# SHATTER THE SKY

## MERRYL TENGESDAL

*Dedicated to:*

*My mom, Norma David, who instilled my hard work ethic.*

*My husband, Kjell, who always supported me on every endeavor.*

*My incredible son, Flynn, and daughter, Maliya, who allow me to provide a positive impact to their lives.*

*Sometimes I yell for you.*

*Sometimes I yell with you.*

*Other times, I yell at you.*

*It doesn't ever change the fact that I am always in your corner.*

- Merryl Tengesdal

# CONTENTS

## Part Two
# GOLD WINGS

**Part Three**

# SILVER WINGS

**Part Four**
# THE NEXT MISSION

# FOREWORD BY PHIL KEOGHAN

Merryl Tengesdal has the most extraordinary and unique resume that we've ever seen from a contestant on the show *Tough As Nails*. From her background as a helicopter pilot, and then as the first and only black woman to fly the U2 aircraft, which fly twice as high as a commercial jet, we knew she was the real deal and perfect for *Tough As Nails*.

As soon as I met her, I knew Merryl would bring strength not only to the individual competition, but also to the team. She is unflappable and it became obvious very quickly that the military had instilled in Merryl a sense of camaraderie and loyalty to her teammates.

As I got to know her personally, I saw that the strength that she portrays on the outside, runs deep. Inside that 'tough as nails' exterior, is a huge and giving heart. Merryl showed up as a tough competitor who came to win, but she was also the first person to lend a hand when one of her teammates was down. She showed up each and every day with a commitment to succeed, and would keep working until her body gave up.

Merryl epitomizes what it means to be on *Tough As Nails*. She has pure grit, is not afraid to take chances and she pushes herself and her team to excel each and every time. Merryl never gives up on herself or her team and will not quit until she gets the job done.

When Merryl asked me to write the foreword of her book, I was honored. I wasn't surprised to learn that her book's title is *Shatter the Sky*. That's what Merryl does.

Phil Keoghan, Host and Executive Producer *Tough As Nails* and *The Amazing Race.*

# INTRODUCTION

With my military background, as a retired pilot, and as a personal trainer, I thought I had a tough background. But nothing prepared me for the experience I was about to go through in the show *Tough As Nails*.

After 23-and-a-half years in the military, where I was indoctrinated into the world of heavily classified, top-secret missions, it was a strange phenomenon for me to promote myself on social media. Everything in my background taught me to keep it under wraps. In the military, and as a U2 pilot, we were dissuaded from using social media. In the U2 community we keep everything very quiet. What we do is very top-secret, a lot of the things we did were classified, so my social media presence was very limited.

When I became a personal trainer, I had to get into the world of social media. When I got on Instagram and Facebook, I decided to put myself out there with this persona that motivates through training. The reason I wanted to do that is I wanted to show people that you don't have to train for a specific event, or to lose weight; you train to be a holistically healthy person – mentally, emotionally, and physically.

I began to introduce some of my family life and my daily struggles to my social media pages. I'm human too, I have my challenges just like everyone else, but the military had instilled some discipline in me, and I wanted to pass that on, teach some techniques.

I got a job at a local sports club and brought boxing for fitness to the club. I have done martial arts since I was 19, and it's really a part of me. It helps center me; it helps ground me. I have done everything from jeet kune do to Kung fu, to Muay Thai, to boxing.

I'm not a morning person, but one morning I had an early fitness class. Before the ladies arrived at the gym, to get in the mood, I put on Lizzo's *Like a Girl*, and began to dance. I was just feeling myself, having fun and recording it on video. I decided to post it on Instagram and Facebook.

Next thing I knew, a woman reached out to me on social media scouting me to be on this show – *Tough As Nails*. At first, I was skeptical, I thought she was trying to scam me. She later told me that her curiosity was piqued because she had seen me dancing, but when she looked at my wall – and saw my military background, my personal history, my family life - she knew I was unique. On the show, they often referred to me as a unicorn – you don't see many black, female military pilots, especially not U2 pilots, or retired Colonels.

After an extensive interview process, I got to be on the second season of *Tough As Nails*. The premise of the show is that there are two teams who compete against each other, while still competing individually. The teammates are 12 everyday working people, from the "Blue-collar" trades. The challenges are not just physically tough, but mentally tough. You need to have grit. You need to be disciplined. Whatever the obstacle is in that challenge, you have to give one hundred percent. Because some of the challenges involved situations I had never done, I had to look at the challenge and give it everything I had.

What I love about the show is that there were no eliminations of the contestants. The idea is that no one goes home. So, you get to see people's stories, how they got to be where they are.

Sitting in the *Tough As Nails* casting trailer, one of twelve cast members from different backgrounds and walks of life, I thought about the many paths we all followed to end up on this blue-collar, everyday hero, backbone of America, reality show.

We were individuals, we were teammates, we were competitors, and we were motivated to overcome the obstacles and accomplish the tasks, dreamt up for us. We had that much in common. But I was sure that no one else had started out in the Bronx with dreams of being an astronaut, studied electrical engineering in college, gone on to Navy officer candidate school, flown helicopters on deployments in the southern hemisphere, piloted Air Force U2s that grazed the edge of space, worked in the five-sided building where majors answered phones for generals, and traveled to parts of the globe that never heard of Starbucks.

The skill set that resulted from that path is certainly eclectic. It grew not only from my experience but also from personal traits such as competitiveness, self-discipline, and the ability to maintain focus in adversity and under pressure. The skills I brought to *Tough As Nails* would not have developed from any other journey, nor would they have been as practical in any other career.

Well, maybe one other. I realize that if I had made a few different decisions, I could have been an immensely successful white-collar, cyber-hacking, criminal. There were times in my life when I might have taken that divergent path, applied my skills and determination for less admirable ends, and ended up in a completely different reality show. If I had not had a few people in my life redirecting me, or seeing my potential, I might have gotten into a lot of mischief. I mentioned this to Nancy, one the show's consultant in the wardrobe trailer, and she just laughed.

*A little mischief never hurt nobody, but I use my powers for good.*

My life began far from this reality show.

Today, I'm a successful personal trainer, a mom, a wife, a pilot, and a retired colonel from the military. But my early life could have taken me on a very different path.

I was born and raised in the Bronx. A black girl, from Co-op City.

My mother and father wanted my name to begin with "M." If I was a boy, I'd have been Marcus. They couldn't agree on a middle name, despite extensive argument, so I don't have one. If I would have had a middle name, it may have been – "Merryl, Settle Down", because that's what I heard most often.

But I simply would not "Settle Down".

I simply would not settle down in my ambitions.

I simply would not settle down in my dreams.

I simply would not settle down in my career.

I simply would not settle down in my marriage.

I simply would not settle down as a mother.

I simply don't believe any one should ever "settle down".

That's why the name of this book is so important to me. We've heard the phrase so much in the last few years – "break the glass ceiling". I'm not a big fan of that phrase. I believe that ceilings are very low. To me, breaking glass ceilings, is a very low bar to hit.

I wrote this book to give little girls and boys, who were told to "settle down", the message that they should aim beyond the sky.

This book is a collection of short vignettes that shaped my experience. The people close to me know that I keep a low profile, I don't share the details of my life easily. I'm a very private person. I give off a tough exterior, but I'm a big softie on the inside. I share these stories from my life to show that I'm no different from you. I have my challenges, my failures, my idiosyncrasies. After all, I am human.

My hope for you, reading this book, is that you take away a perspective, a point of view, or some positive momentum, and apply it as a Life Lesson.

While this book may be *about* me, I wrote this book *for* you.

In my life, it's always been about blasting past the sky and into space. As a U2 pilot, I'd get up beyond the sky and upwards.

I believe when we impose those limitations on ourselves, we create our own limitations.

I believe that there are no limits.

The sky is not the limit.

I believe we should all Shatter the Sky.

Part One

# THE GIRL FROM THE BRONX

# CO-OP CITY

*Strive to be the person kids look up to.*

THE FIRST HOME I ever knew, and the one my mother still lives in, is a two-bedroom, one-bath apartment in Co-op City in the Bronx. Thirty-five high rises and seven townhouse clusters sprawl over 320 acres between I-95 and the Hutchinson River. It is the largest public housing project ever built, accommodating up to 60,000 residents. Co-op City has K-12 schools, shopping centers, professional services, parking garages, playgrounds, parks, and its own zip code. There was a big sandbox in front of our building. I was not allowed to stray from there - my mom watched me from our third-floor balcony.

It was hard for me to stay contained to that sandbox.

In Co-op City, you were either black or Jewish. It was an interesting mix of cultures. I was a black girl, but culturally, I didn't see myself as any different than the Jewish kids. I learned a few Yiddish terms. *Schmuck, Yenta,* and *Mazel Tov,* came up a lot. The Bronx was a melting pot, where cultures intertwined and mingled together.

Everybody knew everybody, people watched out for each other. People were outside on park benches, walking or riding bikes on the greenway. It was as safe as a community in the Bronx could be. From elementary school through high school, I never took a bus - it was always a five minute walk to school.

There was an elderly Jewish woman always at her window watching life go by. She was friendly, always engaging my mom in conversations. She was like a freelance grandmother. She knew the kids in the building and knew who their parents were. We couldn't get away with anything. She was ready to report on any of us kids doing something wrong. She was like the neighborhood hawk that watched over all the kids. She was always perched at the window of her second-floor apartment, calling out to us kids with her faded European accent, as we passed by. I knew, if I got into any mischief, she would see. Worse than that, she would tell my mother. In my mind, I called her Mrs. Hawk, because she saw everything.

If I passed her with my mom, she would say, "Oh, I've got something for you." Then she'd go inside and come out with a butterscotch candy, or a mint, or maybe a nickel. The mints and nickels were great, but I didn't like butterscotch.

I never want to be that old person. You'll never catch me giving out butterscotch candy. Kids want Fun Dip; they don't want butterscotch.

Now my son Flynn comes into my office and sees a Fun Dip on my desk. He asks if he can have it. I tell him, "No, it's mine." But by the time I get to my desk at the end of the day I've already hit my calorie limit, so I have to save it for the next day. I've had that Fun Dip on my desk for a year-and-a-half. That discipline was instilled by Mrs. Hawk.

Another thing that lady instilled in me, is a sense of community. A sense that someone is always looking out for me - whether I was being good or bad. A sense that someone is always watching, so I'd better make the right choice.

Discipline and a deep sense of community have been my two driving factors for my life. They were the instrumental values, engrained in me by my childhood in Co-op City.

## THE CLASS CLOWN

I was always a mouthy kid. Discovering the ability to make other kids laugh opened a new door. Maybe I just wanted the attention. My first kindergarten report card assessed me this way: "Merryl is just a big old chatterbox." But there was hope in the next comment: "She is beginning to exercise more self-control."

Getting laughs was the easy part. The self-control would take a little longer.

One time in kindergarten, I was being a class clown. The teacher had had enough, so she said, "You go sit over there." "Over there" at that moment was where other kids were waiting to go to their special ed class, which is what we called the classes for kids who needed extra help, back in those days.

Suddenly, my whole future flashed before my eyes, and it wasn't the path I had imagined. I was thinking, "Merryl, you have gone and screwed up now." I started bawling because I thought I had been reassigned to special ed class. One of the teachers saw me and asked, "What's wrong?" I can't remember what I told her, but she put me back in the regular class. That's when I realized, at age five, I had to dial it back.

*The more people doubted me or placed limits on me,*
*the more resolved I became to prove them wrong.*

Society expected young females to be a dainty girl in a cute dress playing with Barbies. That was not my idea - Ken, the Dream House, all those stupid ass dolls. They're inanimate objects. Barbie didn't even have bendable arms. GI Joe had joints, you could bend his arms–that was dope. All you could do with Barbie is change her clothes.

Girls were not supposed to trade baseball cards or play sports, which is what I did. You give me a glove and put a ball in my hand, or you need somebody for kickball, I'm down. In kindergarten, they asked us all what we wanted to be when we grew up. I said, "I want to be a baseball player or a soldier."

They kept asking that question through elementary school. By third grade they had a chart that asked the same question, with multiple choice answers separated by gender. Boys had six exciting choices--Fireman, Policeman, Soldier, Baseball Player, Astronaut, and Cowboy. There was no Astronaut box on the girls' side. Our choices sucked. Mother, Nurse, School Teacher, Airline Hostess, Model or Secretary. There was also a blank choice where you could fill in what you wanted to be as an adult. So, I checked that box and wrote in, "Myself".

## SUMMER IN THE CITY

Summers in the Bronx are hot and humid. Sometimes the city would open the fire hydrants so the kids could cool off. One summer, I was nine, and it was super-hot. All the boys were taking their shirts off and tying them around their heads to run through the water. So, I did that. All the girls were mortified. I was nine. I didn't have boobs. I was just hanging with the boys.

Kids would make fun of me for that. They made me feel that my choices to play sports and hang out with the boys were wrong. They called me a tomboy to shame me into making choices that were socially acceptable. For decades, I couldn't say that word without it evoking something deeply unsettling. When I was growing up it was like a curse word to me. It cut pretty deep. They made fun of me until I cried. I hated their guts.

My mom would say, "Go play with so-and-so."

"No."

"Why not?"

"Because they're assholes," is what I was thinking, but I couldn't say that to my mom.

## COMFORTABLE IN MY SKIN

*Black don't crack; even under pressure.*

There are other words I can't say because of the color of my skin. I have trouble even typing them. Throughout history darker skin was a sign of working out in the field, a sign that you're a laborer, not as affluent as others. I got called nasty names. It was bad enough when kids from the building did that, but some of it came from my own family members. They'd think it was funny, that it was a joke. I did not care for it. I still don't.

Growing up, despite all my dreams and aspirations, my self-worth was low. When I was young, self-worth was about being attractive to other people. Appearance was a big part of that. Black people have naturally kinky hair, and I spent a lot of time and effort trying to straighten it with a hot comb to look more like white people. In the 80s, when Jheri Curl came out, I was a victim of that. I tried every type of straightening technique. However, once it grew out, it would break off. My teenage years and young adult years were very frustrating when it came to my hair and choice of style.

Not until I left my Navy sea tour did I go natural. I have never looked back.

Every kid gets frustrated and angry about something. For some, it turns into violence or depression. For me, it was a motivator to become the person I wanted to be. I chose to get back at the kids who ridiculed me by striving and achieving. "I will make you pay with how cool I will become." It was a powerful catalyst to excel.

Now, the older I get the more comfortable I am in my skin. I have a Pakistani friend who is lighter skinned than most Pakistanis. She says, "I don't want to go out in the sun." She doesn't want her skin to get any darker. I say, "Dude, it's Vitamin D, you're ridiculous." In the United States, there's a whole thing between white skin and dark skin. I go out now and lay in the sun all day and get even darker. I think, "Great, I'm going to hit dark purple. Yes. Love it!"

## 2

# THE SOUND OF MUSIC

MY FATHER WAS FROM TRINIDAD. He played keyboards with a band. I inherited his love of music. I remember having a little guitar. I couldn't read notes, but I could strum it. When I was five, the school gave us recorders, a kind of flute. We played "Frere Jacques" to learn to read notes. Throughout my life music has been important. Learning an instrument is a discipline, so that appealed to me. But it also relaxes me and gets me centered when my life departs from controlled flight.

My parents weren't on good terms because my dad stayed out late and spent so much time away. When I was five or six my mom sent me with him to his band practice, maybe thinking that would keep him from straying too far. All I remember is walking in and seeing this glittering array of instruments, one more enticing than the other. It was better than walking into any toy store. I wanted to play every single one of them. But I couldn't. One of the musicians said, "If that kid touches an instrument, she'll break it." So, all I could do is watch and listen.

As soon as I was able to get my hands on a real instrument and play it, I loved it. When I was a teenager, I had this little Casio keyboard. I played hip-hop and stuff. That song from Rocky, with all the trumpets, I can do that one. I did more when I got a bass guitar. I like doing bass riffs. Reading bass is harder because there's bass clef and treble clef. If it's 2/4 time, forget it. Marching music, 7/8, no thanks. I play guitar, bass guitar, keyboard. When I was in school, I played mellophone and French horn.

By the time I was in junior high, I would annoy my classmates, because I could pick up any instrument and play it naturally. I had played trumpet, tenor sax and clarinet well. The other kids in band didn't like that. I'd strum out a five roll. They'd ask, "How do you know this?". I told them to try listening in class. Maybe I sounded smug, but I didn't care.

To this day, I can't pass by an instrument without getting my hands on it.

I play all kinds of instruments. And you know what? I haven't broken one yet.

## THE BEGINNINGS OF MY EXPLORATIONS TO THE BEYOND

The unknown has always had a special appeal to me. Our laundry room was in the basement of the building, and I was beyond supervision down there.

I was beyond the watchful gaze of Mrs. Hawk.

The basements of the separate residential towers were connected by underground corridors–a mysterious labyrinth right beneath my feet! There's a lot of down time while clothes are getting washed. For a little girl who loved exploring the unknown, it was an irresistible attraction. I was adventurous, poking into all the nooks and crannies, discovering what was behind each door, at the end of every hall, around the next corner. I still enjoy corn mazes, but after about an hour, I'm ready to get out.

When I got older, I went to a gym in the neighborhood, and I chose routes that would take me through all these alleys and passages, and I discovered that this exit would take me to one place and that corridor would take me to something else. I enjoyed learning the twists and turns.

How you react to something that you are unprepared for tells you a lot about yourself. Many people try to avoid encounters with the unexpected, but I seek out those opportunities. Certainly, my military career has presented many such occasions, and I look forward to every one of them. The challenge of reacting on the fly to an unanticipated challenge is a rush. Encountering the unknown reveals character.

Sometimes in my explorations, I'd come across a dead roach or a dead rat. I didn't enjoy that. I didn't enjoy the live ones, either. But the dead ones were worse. Anything with skeletons or the dead scared me. Even now, in a scary movie, I cover my eyes. My husband says, "Uncover your eyes." Sometimes I do. Usually not.

*Everything I do is in preparation for the next adventure.*

I don't like gory horror movies. I don't want to sit through a *Friday the 13th* movie and watch a couple making out on a bed until Jason stabs them through the mattress. That's unnecessary. I like supernatural stories and I've always loved sci-fi. I liked the original *Star Trek* and *Space 1999*. Martin Landau back in the day was easy on the eyes.

## ATYPICAL

I think if I had any diagnosis back then, I probably would have been ADD.

I don't know if I was hyper, but, I think at that time the cure for kids who just couldn't sit still was to get a spanking or something to put them in check. I got plenty of those, I didn't die from it.

Was it always pleasant times?

No.

Did I run my mouth a lot in school?

Yes.

But you know, I'm still the person that I am today, so, I appreciate everything my mom has done.

We didn't get diagnosed in those days, but as I think of it, I probably would have been diagnosed with something. It was one of those things that we really didn't have an awareness around.

The way that we dealt in in previous generations, is not like today, with ADHD, all of this is on the rise.

Well, maybe it's on the rise because we're looking to put it into the box called "this". Whereas, back a few generations, a few centuries, a few decades ago, it was just a child that the elders around would look and go - that child needs sports, that child needs martial arts, that child needs to be put into something where they can get some of this curious energy out.

Growing up in that environment worked to my benefit.

My son is a ball of energy too, but I love it. Being a kid like that myself, I know how to channel that. He does soccer, he does jiu jitsu, he does swimming, he does some gymnastics.

We keep him active, keeping his mind active. He is wicked smart.

It's good that I'm his mom and I have that same amount of energy because I know how to deal with that.

## STAR TREK

*I had never seen anyone who looked like me be an astronaut but,
it didn't stop me from trying.*

I was about seven when I got a small, used, black-and-white TV set in my room. It was the kind that you needed to adjust the rabbit ear antenna to pick up one of the available channels. I had to manually pull the power on, wait for the signal, and then turn the dial from a choice of 13 stations. Only three channels got any reception, the rest were grey static. My favorite was the channel that aired *Star Trek*. I would come home from school, grab a snack from the kitchen, throw my backpack on the floor, and sit on my bed to watch. I enjoyed sci-fi because it was all about people exploring the unknown. Of all the *Star Trek* characters I thought Chekov was the most intriguing. Sulu and Chekov were pilot and navigator. Those were the jobs I wanted - controlling where the ship goes. I wanted control of my own ship. I wanted to be an astronaut.

I knew I had to do well in math and science because everyone on *Star Trek* had a science background. I knew I had to be in shape. I knew that I couldn't be a big old donut-eating person and still qualify. I knew I had to go to college because all the characters on *Star Trek* had gone to Star Fleet Academy. And I knew if I wanted to pilot the *Enterprise* that I'd have to become a pilot. It all seemed intuitive to me.

## THE TASTE OF FLIGHT

Most pilot biographies include the first time the subject sees an airplane, touches an airplane, maybe even rides in an airplane. It is a magical moment when the soul of the future aviator is stirred by the wonder of flight and the lure of soaring above the clouds.

I will never forget my first flight. I was six or seven old enough to realize that flying was part of the path to becoming an astronaut. So, I was excited when I found out that my parents were taking me on a plane to Disney World. An elegant jet airliner would whisk us from La Guardia to Florida. It was an extravagant vacation for our family–from the dreary looming towers of Co-op City in the Bronx to the bright, colorful land of Mickey Mouse in sunny Orlando.

In the 1970s airline passenger cabins were still separated into smoking and non-smoking sections. There was no physical barrier, just different seat classifications. Immediately behind the last row of seats in the smoking section was the first row of seats in the non-smoking section.

My mother smoked, so we sat in the smoking section. I had the middle seat between my parents. The narrow, dingy cabin smelled like ass and Cheetos. The nervous fliers in the smoking section lit up and filled the space with noxious fumes. The worst was yet to come.

On the descent, I felt for the first time the pain in my ears that resulted from changing altitude and cabin pressure. I didn't know what was happening or how to relieve the pain, but it became excruciating. I cried and even at that age I had a loud voice. The pain got worse and I got louder. I'm sure the noise caused the smokers to puff harder.

The stewardess (back in the days before we changed the term to the more politically correct term - flight attendant), rushed over. "Would you like some gum?"

*'No. I don't want any of your damn gum. Get away from me. I'm in pain! I need a tranquilizer!'* That's what I wanted to say, but somehow all that came out was a continuous piercing scream that distributed my anguish amongst my fellow passengers.

My parents couldn't do anything to help and all I remember is the smell of cigarette smoke, the intense agony, and this annoying stewardess who kept trying to get me to shut up and stop crying. That was my first experience in an airplane. It sucked. But I was still determined to become a pilot.

## 3

# JUST ME AND MY MOM

By the time I was seven or eight, my dad wasn't around that much, though I think he was still in New York. My parents were divorced by the time I was in eighth grade. They were having issues before that, but when you're a kid you don't realize it until they tell you, "Hey, we're getting a divorce."

I remember asking if it was my fault. "No, it's not your fault." They never say, "Hell yeah, it's your fault. You're causing us stress. We're not having intimacy. You're a pain in the ass."

I think my dad just realized the dad life wasn't for him and he wanted to go. I was not his first child. I was number three. I had two half-brothers I never met, still in Trinidad

My father passed away some time ago. Before he passed, I tried to connect with him, but he simply wasn't a presence in my life. For many years, it was just me and my mom. I didn't know life any other way.

## WORKING WOMEN

After the divorce, my mom picked up a job as a bank teller, then she moved to the post office. She was always hardworking. Most of my friends came from single parent homes. The dad was gone, the mom had to pick up a job.

Maybe that's the reason I did not get married until later in my life. I saw what a bad marriage did to my mom and my friends' moms, and I didn't want to be in that position. For a long time, I didn't think I would get married.

My mom worked the night shift, so I spent a lot of time with my grandmother and sometimes my aunt. My grandmother had her favorite shows – *Benny Hill, Dallas, Falcon Crest* and *Golden Girls*. She showed me how to crochet. I'm still no good at it.

My mother and grandmother both had the same work ethic. They never instructed me to work hard and not give up, but I saw how they lived, and I wanted to be the same way. They never had to tell me, they showed me.

None of the women from that side of the family took any crap from kids. One time I was at my grandmother's house, and she was vacuuming. She said or did something that pissed me off. I said, "Shut up," but I didn't think she could hear me over the noise of the vacuum cleaner. But she did. She freaking snapped that cord and whipped me good. And she was still vacuuming with the other hand when she did it! It was a total ninja move. The whole time she was spanking me I was just hoping that she wouldn't tell my mom because then I'd get spanked again when I got home. Two generations of spanking. I didn't want that. The only upside was that with my dad gone, my mom couldn't use one of his belts to administer punishment.

My grandmother knew I was an explorer. She probably thought it was just a phase. She used to have old transistor radios around. I'd get a screwdriver and take them apart and mess with them. It was electrical. There were capacitors, diodes. I liked looking at the soldered connections. Sometimes I would disconnect something, hook up a battery, and see if it worked. I'd do it for hours. It came full circle in college when I got my degree in electrical engineering.

My grandmother worked in the senior center portion of the community center. I'd go down there with her and hang out with old Jewish people all day. They liked me because I was respectful. We'd do arts and crafts and play bingo. People at the center liked my grandmother. She was always busy. She was a senior citizen working with other senior citizens who weren't as mobile.

## MY FIRST MENTOR

At the Baptist church next door there was an after-school program for kids where you could study or go out to a huge open court and run wild. The after-school section was run by an old black lady. She was tiny, like Yoda, but mean. Not a woman to mess with. She ruled with fear, absolute fear. If you got out of line, she would paddle the crap out of you. I got *rulered* once, which is what we would call it when a teacher hit you with the long end of a ruler. *'Why is this lady hitting me?'* I wondered. But it was probably for not keeping my mouth shut.

When I was nine or ten, mean Miss Yoda was replaced by Miss Harriet. She was a tall, no-nonsense black lady. If kids mouthed off, pushed the boundaries, she would keep them in line, but not out of fear. She still had permission to paddle people, but she was nicer. She had previously been a teacher and she had two kids of her own, but they weren't in the program. She saw that I had an interest in space and science. As a teacher, if you see a kid who's interested in something, you feed that. She brought me *Star Trek* books to read. I think they belonged to her. She even let me keep some of them. She was the first adult who had interests similar to mine and who encouraged me to pursue them.

As my first mentor, Miss Harriet showed me the powerful and lifelong positive effect an adult taking interest in a child can have. That's why I enjoy being a mentor to young people. They are overflowing with potential, and all it takes is a little spark to light their rocket.

Adults should also be aware of the negative effects they can have on an aspiring young person. Some adult once told a young Michael Jordan that he would never be a professional basketball player. He's the greatest of all time. Adults have this stupid ability to shut young people down.

My advice to young people is pursue your passion. Dig in and learn as much about it as you can. Work to understand the concepts. When I started high school, I had an aerodynamics book. At first, when I opened it, I'd see lift, drag, and a lot of other unfamiliar terms. I'd close the book and walk away. But I'd come back to it. Certain concepts are not easy but if you keep studying them you will understand and master them. Once you get it, you'll never forget it. Don't listen to adults who tell you it's never going to happen. They're friggin' idiots.

### PRE-TEEN TURBULENCE

By seventh grade I was reading at the tenth-grade level and doing high school level math. My report card told the rest of the story. "Merryl is a bright girl but must control her behavior in language arts." I was running my mouth too much.

My mom expected a lot from me. She was the biggest positive influence in my life. Twice a year she went to the parent-teacher conferences. If I got an A, she'd want to know why it wasn't an A+. I'd get grounded, yelled at, but it never discouraged me. I never had academic trouble, it was always behavioral problems. I was just a chatty, distracting influence - a smart ass.

Mr. Russo, my junior high school science teacher, was another early mentor. Peter J. Russo was a short white guy, Italian. He was one of the first people in school I just got along with. He liked science, I liked science. He played trumpet, I played trumpet. He would ask me to work for him after school. The science lab was a hot mess. We would talk while we got the lab squared away.

My journal says, "Mr. Russo taught me things I never dreamed of. He acted like a father to me. I wish he was my father, but he already has three sons." With no father figure in my life, I gravitated toward male teachers like Mr. Russo. In school, most of my mentors were white males. Maybe that was because there weren't many black male teachers. I tried to get away with a lot of things in junior high school. Mr. Russo never let me do that.

## ONLY ONE QUEEN BEE

From age thirteen to seventeen, my mom and I clashed. Two strong-willed women, single mother and teenage daughter, sharing an apartment with one bathroom. There was bound to be trouble. There can only be one Queen Bee.

In the summer, I was on a private track team in Co-op City, the Zodiac Track Club. It was started by the coach, Mr. Taylor, for his daughter, Monica, who was an amazing hurdler. I was in ballet class with her, and we'd do an exercise where we would jump over boxes. I could do three or four on a good day. Monica could clear six. So, I joined the track team with Monica and her sister, Carla – the two fastest girls on the team. I thought Monica would go to the Olympics. The Taylors were in Section Four of Co-op City, I was in Section Three. There was always a rivalry between sections.

My mom was going to drive me to the big track meet – the last day of the nationals' competition. Walking over to the parking garage, she was going off about something – I can't even remember what it was. It was the culmination of a lot of things. All I remember was my mom ranting and raving. It was journal worthy: "Today I was almost going to have a fight with my mother. She always thinks she is right even though sometimes she is. She gives me no word to say when we are arguing and when I try to say something she tells me to shut up. But I don't, so she smacks me. Today she tried it again. I moved away and she said, 'Come here.'" She came after me, but I was on the track team. She wasn't going to catch me, that ain't happening. At fourteen, you get smacked by your mom, it's no big deal. But I wasn't going to get smacked that day.

She gave up trying to catch me, so we got in the car. She said, "We'll finish this when you get home." I went silent. Neither of us said anything. She dropped me off at the track meet and just left me.

The event was somewhere in the Bronx. This was the nationals, so there was a huge crowd. But obviously I had a lot on my mind. I didn't even make the finals in javelin and throwing the discus I stepped over the line every time. A triple fault – it was a terrible showing. I'd never done so poorly in my life. The coach was on my case, the assistant coach was on my case. It was a long day.

On top of a disappointing performance, I had to walk home. The whole way I'm thinking the rest of this fight is waiting for me. The track meet was just halftime. I came in, I was sitting in the living room, thinking about my shitty day. My mom came in. "Okay, you ready to fight now?"

I'd been at the track meet all afternoon and I had walked home. I was too tired to fight. Besides, I'm fourteen years old. Why do I want to fight my mom? "No, I don't want to fight."

"That's what I thought." And she walked away. Later I heard her on the phone, talking to a friend. "Yeah, I was going to whip her ass." She was tough, and she wasn't the type to back down. But she never tried to hit me again.

## 4

# TEENAGED TROUBLES

My JOURNAL ENTRIES at the time all had star dates, like Captain Kirk would use when making log entries on *Star Trek*. Yeah, I know that makes me sound like a dork. A typical journal entry would read, "Star Date 8320.1," which in my system meant 1983, 20th day of the 1st month. The salutation would be, "Dear Odex." The name had no significance, I just thought it sounded cool.

I was thinking about my career in one entry:

> *Dear Odex, I wish to become a navigator on the space shuttle. But people on the space shuttle are 45, and I don't want to be on the space shuttle at 45, so technology better speed up.*

The first line in my journal about my first day at Harry S. Truman High school was:

> *Met all my teachers and they're all suckers, except for Mr. Vanduren, biology.*

I tried out for third trumpet in senior band but didn't make the cut. I hadn't played trumpet for two months. This was high school. It was time to play with the big dogs and I sucked.

There was a position open for mellophone, which had keys like a trumpet, but looked like a French horn. It was sort of a hybrid, and I didn't like it. I took up the French horn, which I did like. It's a beautiful instrument.

I had been annoying in junior high because I could pick up any instrument and it came naturally. I had played trumpet, tenor sax and clarinet well. The other kids in band didn't like that. I'd play a tune I had heard once, pitch perfect. They'd ask, "How do you know this?" I told them to try listening in class. Looking back on it now, I was annoying, but I didn't care.

I was in the band and on the bowling team, the softball team, the basketball team, and the math team. I was also a science nerd. The members of those groups don't naturally mesh. I was like the skeleton key who could fit in anywhere.

## THE ISLAND OF MISFIT TOYS

I had many acquaintances, but I usually stuck with a small core group of friends who were intelligent and a little odd – lovable weirdos. We'd go to the Renaissance festival all dressed up. Then we'd get drunk and party. We had friends on the outskirts, but some of them were too much into drugs. One of them overdosed. We were the core group. We didn't judge each other. We'd hang out in each other's houses, or under the building, just chilling and having Seinfeld moments, talking till midnight.

It was an eclectic group, as distinctive as the names we all chose for our role-playing game characters. Sri was a white Jewish girl; she wore Doc Martens all the time and dressed all in black. Galen was Hispanic. Alderon was a Jewish guy from a single parent home who worked while he went to school to support his family. Galen and Alderon were good friends. Argus was a black guy I dated for a while – I learned a lot about relationships from him. Baldafar and Morlas were both wicked smart. They dropped out of school at 16. DM wanted to be a makeup artist, but he lost interest along the way.

You'd see us hanging out as a group, you wouldn't know what to make of us – black people, Jewish people, Hispanic people, some goth, some nerds. We were like the Breakfast Club from the Island of Misfit Toys.

When I was twelve, we started playing Man, Myth and Magic; a role-playing game, before people did that on the internet. Later, in high school, we switched to Dungeons & Dragons. DM was the Dungeonmaster who was in charge of the game. If you have a good Dungeonmaster, the game can be very interesting. We played for several hours a night once a week. We used to do different missions. We had to work as a group, fighting wraiths and dragons, looking for treasures, exploring the unknown.

You can create your own character. I had a druid elf character I played for years. Her name was Drakiel. She was one with animals, different than the usual thief, elf, wizard, warrior. It takes a long time to develop your character and you work hard to raise your character to a higher level. Just like real life.

I'd love to go hang out with them again, but we all have our lives. They're all doing well in their respective lives.

I still talk to Robin, AKA Sri. She lives in Vermont. We've been friends since kindergarten. We're two people from the same place who went in totally different directions.

## LOSING MY RELIGION

I'm a recovering Roman Catholic. I played in a music trio at church – violin, flute, and me on clarinet. I was an altar server, wore the robes and did the whole thing. But Roman Catholics won't allow women become altar servers.

I was an alter server for a while until the rules changed banning girls from being alter servers. I remember being upset, confronting the priest of the church. After I was told there was nothing he could do, I walked away. I could not understand why the rules changed on a dime. It didn't make sense to me. At that time I was probably around ten, or eleven.

I said, "That's stupid", and I walked away.

When I was sixteen, I returned to church for my Confirmation classes. A nun was teaching us about how premarital sex was bad, and abortion was bad. I whispered to my friend, "She probably wouldn't think abortions were bad if she got raped." Unfortunately, the nun overheard me and I got kicked out of class.

The reason I made the comment was to not be disrespectful. I was frustrated that a nun was telling me what was right and wrong in this type of situation. There was no allowance to think anything different. There was no room for debate. You either believe this way or there is something wrong with you. Not the type of people or organization I would ever want to align myself with; at any age.

I'm not a churchgoer. When you go to these churches now, they're the size of a college campus, you think you're going to pray. Then this full band comes out and they're playing Earth, Wind, and Fire. No, I can't do it. It's a personal preference. And they all start saying, "Praise Jesus." I get scared. It's not my scene. If I did go to church, it would be quiet, monotone. That's what recovering Roman Catholics are used to.

I believe in a higher existence. If you want to call it "God," that's up to you. I don't ascribe to this belief that God will do things for you. As I get older, I think it's more about opportunities that you take or don't take. A lot of people believe in God and believe in miracles. To me, sometimes the timing is just right.

## THE LONE WOLF

I went to a Christian sleep away camp one summer when I was 15 or 16. The awesome part was that they had ATVs and bows and arrows.

They taught that if you didn't believe in God, you'd go to hell. So I asked, "What if you're a Buddhist, and all you know is Buddhism, and you have no idea of God? Would God be so pissed off that he would send you to hell?" They had no answer for that. I thought, "Maybe God is just who you think he is."

But it made me think about religion. There was a counselor there, not much older than I was. We had a talk. I told him I was questioning some things. I trusted him with thoughts I usually don't share. As far as I was concerned, that was a conversation between me, him and God. But immediately after that talk, he told all the other counselors about it. All of a sudden, they were coming up to me and talking about my private thoughts.

I was shocked, embarrassed and pissed off. I completely shut down. As soon as people tried to start a conversation about my beliefs, I just walked away. I told myself that I'd never make that mistake again. It cut me to my core. It was even hard to write about in my journal. I can write about anything–dreams, family troubles, sex, whatever. But that one, you have to sigh between every letter that you write. It was just painful. I have this thing about people getting in my business. If I feel betrayed, I just shut off, I close that door and move on.

People at the camp didn't know why I wouldn't talk.

They said, "You're a lone wolf type of person."

That was funny because I have two cousins who are incredibly talented artists. One cousin does comic books now which are very popular. I used to love looking at their sketch books. When I got cards from them, they were individual works of art. They would teach me how to draw. My cousin Eddie created a character, a beautiful wolf, which was also an acronym for "Warrior of Limitless Fury."

I used to draw that character. I was an angry child, a loner, and a warrior. I identified with that character. People who knew me back then would see a picture of a wolf and say, "That's Merryl."

## WARRIOR OF LIMITLESS FURY

One lone wolf decision I made was to take summer classes at our rival high school, Evander. It wasn't required, I just wanted to do something with my summer. Most of the other students had to be there to repeat classes they hadn't passed in regular session. Evander at that time was probably one of the most violent high schools in the Bronx. There were a lot of stabbings, and guns were just coming in. They had metal detectors. I knew if they found out I was a Truman student, I'd be a target. I remember one kid who had been mouthing off all summer until the teacher finally had enough. They started arguing and then they came to blows. It was a real fist fight, clearing tables and everything. The teacher beat the student's ass. It was glorious.

Not so glorious was an incident that involved my friend Victoria, a girl in the building whom I bowled with. She was friends with a guy named Craig.

There are several journal pages devoted to a plan they dreamed up for prom.

Looking back on those journals entries, I can feel the pain of the words I wrote in my journal:

> They wanted to use me for getting back at this guy Trig. It was Craig's scheme, but Victoria helped him.

Back in the day before cell phones and Zoom, you could arrange for a three-way conference call using land lines. This was how the conspiracy was planned. I don't recall the details of the scheme, but judging from the journal entry, it involved the prom and an elaborate disguise.

> They wanted me to buy a wig, wear makeup, use a different name, wear glasses and high heels. And they said if I go to prom, don't talk about sports or anything.

I didn't want any part of this, and I didn't want to pretend to be someone I was not, especially if I had to dress like a hooker. I told them I didn't want to be involved and hung up. At least, I thought I hung up. I pressed down on the button that ends the call, but it did not break the connection. I could still hear them talking, but they thought I was gone. This part I remember like it was yesterday...

*Craig said I sounded like a man on the phone. I was hurt but what really killed me was that Victoria was laughing. I'm very mad that I cried over it and I don't usually get that mad. It wasn't their planning that I was mad at. I was mad at what they were trying to make me look like.*

Making fun of me for sounding or acting like a man pushed all my buttons. I was so upset that I was still crying when my mom came home.

"What is happening?" When I told my mom what I'd heard, she was pissed. She called Victoria's mom. Victoria came down to apologize, crying, not because she was sorry, but because her mom chewed her ass. We had been friends before. When you're a teenager and someone does that, it's a betrayal. When people made fun of me, they're dead to me. When she did that, I thought - "All right, I got your number." I just had to remember that she'll get what she deserves in the end.

Anger about what happened to me when I was younger can be great motivational fuel. The best revenge is a life well lived.

# 5
# IT TAKES A VILLAGE

WHEN I WAS FIFTEEN, Miss Harriet gave me a binder that listed all these programs available in the state that kids can apply to. It listed all the requirements--whether they were looking for girls, disadvantaged youth, a certain GPA. I showed my mom and she said, "Pick some stuff and we'll apply and see what happens." Miss Harriet encouraged me to apply for the Science Technology Entry Program, STEP. They took a whole bunch of kids up to State University of New York, Binghamton. We did math courses, biology, organic chemistry--for some reason I was crushing organic chem. The following year selected kids were invited back to do actual research under faculty supervision.

Junior year I went to the Bronx High School of Science. I took genetics because I remembered the episode of *Star Trek* where the villain Khan emerges from cryogenic suspension, a product of late twentieth century genetic research. I learned about fruit flies – they only have four chromosomes, so it simplifies the research. I realize as I talk about this, I sound more and more like a nerd.

## CHALLENGER

A lot of kids who were interested in science also wanted to be astronauts. Then the space shuttle *Challenger* exploded. After that, many of those kids didn't want to be astronauts anymore. Americans had never had a death in space. The Apollo 1 fire was on the pad. A friend I grew up with, also from a single parent household, shared my goal of going into space. We talked to each other and discussed how we felt about what happened with the *Challenger*.

We both agreed, "That just means that there are a million fewer kids who want to be astronauts now, so our chances just got better. The pool of competitors is smaller."

Nothing was going to deter us.

Fast forward to 2011 when I met Air Force General Richard Scobee, a one-star at the time. He was the son of Dick Scobee, the commander of *Challenger*. We brushed that topic and I felt bad then about what I thought. He had watched his father die in front of his eyes. As an adult and a parent, I see that from a different perspective. General Scobee is a three-star now, chief of Air Force Reserve Headquarters.

The crew of the *Challenger* died doing something they loved. They were doing something awesome. It was quick. They probably had just enough time to say, "Oh, shit," and it was over. The *Challenger* incident didn't deter me because going into space was what I wanted to do. Life is all about trying to do something positive. When your number is called, it's called. There's nothing you can do about it. I'd rather go that way than have some murderers come after me. In the afterlife, if I died in some stupid way, I'd be pissed. But if I was flying a U2 and some freak thing happened, I'd be okay with that. It's a high-risk mission, a mission very few are entrusted to take on, and I know the risks. If I died doing that, I'm good. I'd think - *Damn, I went up in a blaze of glory.*

## BLAZE OF GLORY

My academic career almost went up in a blaze of glory. During senior year I had a lot of idle time since I had already fulfilled most of my requirements to graduate. I only needed English, social studies and gym – those three classes were the last requirements. I had a lot of down time. I would take shorthand and baking, all these stupid classes. I got kicked out of band because I threatened a teacher. I was just out of control.

Our high school had a little Indian museum – today we'd call it a Native American museum, or maybe Indigenous People museum. I don't know what the current term is because of the shifting sands of political correctness. I love indigenous people because they are the foundation of society. But I don't keep up with the latest PC lingo. Black people might be African Americans or people of color now, but "black" is just a lot shorter and easier to write.

Our school also had a planetarium and a little theater for performances and presentations. Other schools would come to ours to use those facilities. We had about 2000 students at Harry S. Truman High. The planetarium was run by Steven Lieb, an administrator who had an office at our school but also worked in the wider district. Since I was a science nerd, I got to know him through the planetarium program. He could have ended my high school career very quickly because of one final escapade.

I applied to be part of the Planetarium Squad, students who helped run the presentations. I think I irritated Terry Buchalter, one of the faculty members, because I got a little too enthusiastic. They had all this electrical equipment that I just couldn't keep my hands off of. I wanted to examine and take apart every component.

I was just so excited, but he said, "Merryl, you gotta settle down."

He said something to Mr. Lieb and Lieb talked to me. "I hear you're quite the whirlwind."

I think Lieb talked him into letting me continue. We would do cool stuff like solder circuits, all very hands on. And I got my own key to the building because the Planetarium Squad also did the lighting for shows in the little theater. During the weekends they would pay you five bucks an hour to light the show. Back then that was a lot of money. But the money paled in comparison to having keys to the school.

There was a big fashion show coming up. I was assigned to light the show, so I had total access to the building that night. I recruited my friends Sri and Janice. Academically, Janice was ranked third in the class, I was in the top ten percent, and Sri was just getting by. Sri and Janice had one thing in common–they weren't interested in theatrical lighting. But that's not why I recruited them.

Harry S. Truman High School was a seven-story building with elevators and stairwells. But the student elevators were always breaking down. The teachers' elevator always worked. I had gym class on the ground floor and the very next class was math, on the seventh floor. When the elevator wasn't working, it was a Stairmaster sprint to make it to class. The teachers' elevator had a key lock – only teachers were permitted to use it. This injustice cried out for correction.

Our school had a crime problem, so security cameras had been installed in the corridors and stairwells. But I had inside knowledge of that system, including not only the locations of the cameras but also which ones were working, and which ones were not. I devised a route carefully to avoid the working cameras. Our target was the teachers' elevator locks. The concept was flawless, and I had my accomplices. We executed the plan the night of the fashion show.

. . .

I had planned to use Krazy Glue, but I also knew that there was a Krazy Glue solvent. I built a lot of plastic models at the time, so I also brought plastic model cement. So we squeezed Krazy Glue into the elevator locks and covered them with plastic model cement. It could be classified as a chemistry project.

But once you get access to the entire school and you've defeated the security cameras and you have your crew and the proper combination of adhesives, you hate to stop after gluing just the elevator locks. We decided also to glue the locks of our least favorite classes.

In the military, this is known as "mission creep".

Still avoiding the functioning security cameras, we glued the locks of our most hated classrooms. But then I thought that if the faculty decided to cross-reference the classes with the students in those classes, they could narrow down the list of suspects. Therefore, purely as a defensive measure, I thought we should glue the locks of classrooms we never went into and had no connection to, just to throw them off the track. Wouldn't I have made a great white collar criminal?

The next day, the teachers were pissed. It was a spectacular crime, executed masterfully, and the whole school was talking about it. Sri thought if they found out, they wouldn't let us graduate.

Naturally, you can't pull off something spectacular and not take credit for it. I was bragging. That was my downfall. Mr. Lieb called me over and did a casual interrogation. "What do you think of what they did to the locks?"

All I could say was, "What locks?" And he just looked at me with those narrow eyes, and I knew that he knew. But he let it all go away, never said anything to anybody. I didn't get in trouble, my friends didn't get in trouble. I think the statute of limitations is expired, so I guess it's okay to tell it here. Since there were no severe consequences, I could have been tempted to continue a life of crime. But now I use my powers for good.

## THE BRONX BOWLERS

One of my last adventures before leaving for college was a bowling tournament. There were prizes of scholarship money for the top three teams - $1000 for first, $500 second and $250 for third. Teams were either father-son or mother-daughter. My mom and I were good bowlers. And we were both competitive.

The tournament was a single elimination - when you lost a game, you were out. It was held in Queens, one of five boroughs in New York, of which the Bronx was one. There were certain rivalries between boroughs. Queens had the airports and Shea Stadium. The Bronx just had a reputation for rough neighborhoods and rough people. So when my mom and I rolled up from the Bronx, not much was expected of us.

What the other contestants didn't know was that my mom had been bowling in two or three leagues for as long as I can remember, at Gun Post Lanes in the Bronx. It's still there. I went with her on those nights, so the bowling alley was my second home. At first, I'd be in the child center with other little kids whose parents bowled in the league. It was just a big room with video games, so I'd get quarters to play Asteroids while my mom bowled.

By the time I was eight, I was bowling in a league. I got to know the manager. He took me behind the lanes and showed me how the pin-setting machines worked. The lanes were real wood back then, and I watched as they oiled them and learned how they were maintained. Wooden lanes have a distinctive sound, completely different from the current synthetics and composite wood products they use now. It got so that I could tell if a ball was going to hit the pocket just by the sound it made on the lane. I lived, breathed, and ate bowling alleys. At one time, I thought I'd like to be the manager of a bowling alley.

· · ·

By the time of the tournament, I carried a 155-160 average, and hit 200 fairly often. My mom and I were determined and focused and we surprised a lot of people. By the end, first and second place were sewed up and two teams were fighting for third–ours and a father and son from Queens. They were the home team, and we were challenging them on their own turf.

I don't know if it was a female/male thing, a black/white thing, or a Bronx/Queens thing, but the competition was intense. Putting us on adjacent lanes didn't do anything to diminish the intensity. One game would decide who would take third and who would go home empty handed. As you know, my mom is tough and doesn't back down. I certainly did not intend to lose. It was pretty close right up to the seventh frame, then we took the lead and never lost it. We won the $250 scholarship and took it back home to the Bronx. The father and son team from Queens left with nothing but pissed off expressions.

## THE HARLEM SHUFFLE

My mom was born in Harlem, then moved to the Bronx. She never really left the city. Maybe she'd make a trip here and there, but she stayed. The rest of my family - grandma, aunt, cousin - never ventured out after that (although my cousin went to law school in Louisiana). They all still live within half a mile of each other. That's not me. I feel like I always got things to do. There are some people who are content to stay on the twenty-yard line. I want to make touchdowns.

I left because the Bronx was stifling. I love the Bronx for what it has–the diversity, the culture. Like the song says about New York, "If you can make it there you can make it anywhere." All the other boroughs have gentrified. The neighborhoods have improved, housing values have gone up, new businesses have moved in. But the Bronx is still savage. It refuses to comply. It's cutthroat. People are brutally honest with you. I like that. But I wanted a change, and I wanted a challenge.

Freedom as a kid was getting out and doing. It wasn't because my mom and I didn't get along. It's just that I'm a person of action. Inaction is something that's hard for me. I gotta be moving the ball forward. I have to identify an objective and keep going.

I was ready to live life and do something, as this journal entry shows: *I'm sick of the house I live in, sick of the earth period. I long for the stars and the adventure of the unknown. And I've got none of it. I wish there was someone called Kirk, Spock, McCoy, or Chekov who could take me away from this planet. Wish I had a little bit of adventure. Wish I did not have to take all these unnecessary courses.*

After I joined the military, my mom would ask me, "Are you coming back to New York?"

I'd tell her, "No", but what I was thinking was - "Hell, no, I'm not coming back. Why would I want to come back?"

A couple of people from Co-op City reached out to me recently. They're still living in the same building from thirty years ago. My mom has been there fifty years. If I were still living in the Bronx, I'd kill myself. Maybe not in the physical sense, but I'd be sitting on the couch smoking pot because I'd be so damned depressed. Not that the Bronx is a bad place to live, but what would I be doing? A 9 to 5 job? I couldn't even imagine that.

Once you live outside the apartment, it's hard to go back to a place where people are living on top of you. The only reason I'd want to go back is to be nostalgic and eat the pizza I remember when I was growing up. I want to go someplace new. There's freedom in that.

# 6

# A NEW STATE OF MIND

I HAD BEEN ACCEPTED at the University of New Haven, a private college in Connecticut, about 80 miles from New York City. It was an hour and a half by Metro train. Okay, not a long way from home, but at least it was a different state.

New Haven had an engineering school. I was torn between aerospace engineering and aeronautical engineering. Aerospace is more about mechanical issues, but aeronautical is about airplanes, and I was fascinated by airplanes. As it turned out, I did neither of those and chose to study electrical engineering. You could do either analog, which is all about building power grids, or you could do digital processing, which is about signal processing, designing computers, things like that. I chose digital processing because it was interesting and a solid degree to fall back on if the astronaut plan failed to launch. I already had experience thanks to the summer STEP program at Binghamton and my grandma's transistor radios.

The University of New Haven is a Division Two school, quiet, maybe underestimated, but expanding its boundaries all the time. They have a marina and they're opening up marine studies program. University of New Haven is a diamond in the rough. And they party like nobody's business. It was a school that reminded me of myself.

College is when I began to study martial arts. There was a jeet kune do place right down the street. Jeet kune do was Bruce Lee's approach. It means "Way of the Intercepting Fist." Martial arts is not only about fighting, but also about physical conditioning, discipline, philosophy and focus.

Focus was something I was lacking. Besides jeet kune do, I was taking 18 to 20 credit hours, I was doing a work study program, I was a walk-on for the basketball team, and I was in ROTC. I wasn't missing out on the social side of college either. It was a great place to make friends, meet guys, drink, and party. But I was burning the candle at both ends and heating up in the middle.

I had a friend who was a civil engineering major. We were in the same class my second semester. She'd look over and see me sleeping during the lecture. Every once in a while, I'd open my eyes, raise my hand, and most astounding of all, ask a pertinent question. The professor would answer, and as soon as he turned back to the lecture, I'd close my eyes and go back to sleep. She laughs about that to this day. But the result was an unimpressive academic record.

## ON THE RIGHT TRACK

Our basketball team didn't usually travel, but we did make a trip to California for some exhibition games. It was the first time I'd been on an airplane since our family trip to Disney World, and the familiar piercing agony of pressure in my ears had not diminished. I realized that I could not be a pilot if this continued. By trial and error, I figured out how to equalize the pressure on the return trip. That was a major obstacle out of the way.

Keeping the pilot goal in mind, I avoided other potential hurdles on the astronaut track. I went home for holidays, spring break and summer. It was great hanging out on the roof with my friends. Some of them were pot smokers. I had no idea what kind of drug tests the military had, so whenever the marijuana came out, I said, "I'll be back when you're done," and left. I didn't want to open that door and risk being disqualified. My goal was to get a lot higher than that.

My freshman physics professor at New Haven was Dr. Morrison. He was a white guy, the only professor on campus who taught nuclear physics. He received a lot of threats because the anti-nuke crowd thought he was teaching people how to make bombs. We were talking one day in his classroom, and I noticed that his lab area was a hot mess. I offered to help him get it under control, so I got into a work study program with him.

## SUMMER IN MAINE

We got to be friends and in my junior year he told me about a summer program at the University of Maine doing experiments in thin film deposition. I knew nothing about that, and it didn't sound very interesting.

He urged me to apply. "We're going to hone those skills you've got."

"I'm not doing it."

"You gotta do it."

"I don't want to."

"You're doing it."

I did it. I applied and was accepted. Dr. Morrison drove down to the Bronx from Connecticut, picked me up, and drove me up to the University of Maine. He had four daughters, and he treated me like one of them.

Thin film deposition is a vacuum technique used to deposit very thin metallic layers on a slide. Then we measured differences in conductivity with different thicknesses of metallic film. We used tungsten, and when I say very thin, we're talking nanometers.

The vacuum device that placed the tungsten layers on the slide used a sputtering system, and the nozzle got clogged after a while. I worked with a graduate student who was more experienced than I was. He remarked that we'd have to clean the system soon, but he had made very clear to me that I wasn't to touch the equipment when he was not there to supervise.

Touching equipment was an urge I was never able to resist, especially when unsupervised. When the grad student was gone, I spoke to a professor about cleaning the system and he was glad to show me the technique. I cleaned the system thoroughly and when the grad student came back and said it was time to perform that task, I said, "Already done."

He didn't believe me at first, but after inspecting the system, he saw that it had been restored to optimal condition. But instead of being impressed or at least grateful, he was mad. "I told you not to touch anything!"

I explained that I'd consulted a professor, learned how to service the system, and performed the task. He eventually settled down and we had a good working relationship. The experiments we were doing back then were pure research, but now those techniques are used in solar cells, LEDs, printed circuits, optical coatings, all kinds of applications. It was a great opportunity that I would have missed if Dr. Morrison hadn't pushed me.

## IN THE NAVY

*Most journeys are not a straight path.*
*Be prepared for the detours.*

Becoming a military pilot was still my top priority, and I thought ROTC would give me an edge when it came time to join the service. There was no Navy ROTC program at New Haven, so I joined the Air Force ROTC. I stayed in for two years–there were classes, drills, all kinds of military preparatory activities. The other students in ROTC were proper, circumspect, and mild mannered–the kind of people you don't usually meet in the Bronx. It wasn't a good fit for me. I knew these were not the people I wanted to fly and fight with.

The Air Force officer candidate program did not guarantee that you become an Air Force pilot–that would be determined after you were in the program. The Navy allowed officer candidates to choose aviation going in as long as they passed the necessary tests. I had also missed the cut-off for the Air Force Officer Qualifying Test and had trouble with the eye test. It seemed I was not destined to serve in the United States Air Force.

## WHITE COLLAR "CRIME"

*Success didn't come without struggle.*

My studies were hampered by self-inflicted distractions. I was kicked off the school computer system for broadcasting inappropriate material. And I lost my work study gig for forging a timecard. It was not technically embezzling because I was going to make up the hours, but I needed the money. I like to think of it as an advance on my wages, but they didn't see it that way.

When I was a kid, my dad had been involved in a scam that involved revenue from toll booths. He was caught, but he rolled over and informed on the other people who were involved, so he didn't get charged. I knew I had that propensity and realized that forgery was not the path to the stars. This is probably where I veered off the road that led to white collar crime.

My academics suffered and I failed a class during my junior year. Whatever path I chose to become a military pilot, I knew that a college degree was a necessary achievement. I buckled down on the academics as a senior and graduated with a degree in electrical engineering.

## THE BLUE ANGELS

My boyfriend at the time had enlisted in the Navy and he was in Pensacola. I made a trip down there to visit him. Pensacola is home to the Navy Flight Demonstration Squadron, better known as the Blue Angels. The Naval Aviation Museum is also there, and it is very impressive. There's an exhibit that honors all the naval aviators who became astronauts. I met a security guard who was doing his rounds. His name was Bacon. We started talking about flying for the Navy. He said it's easy to land on land, but it takes real skill to land on a ship at sea. There seemed to be a lot of signs pointing me toward the Navy.

Up to that point, I was trying to find a military program for enlisted personnel to become pilots. Air Force and Navy pilots are officers, but in the Army, warrant officers, who are enlisted, fly helicopters. I took the Armed Services Vocational Aptitude Battery (ASVAB) test which tells the military what you might be suited to. I scored high for aviation.

My Navy boyfriend was now stationed in Yuma, Arizona, which, I realize, is a long way from an ocean. But there's a Marine Corps Air Station in Yuma, and Yuma is part of the San Diego Navy Recruiting District. My boyfriend told me that the Navy recruiter in San Diego was looking for aviation candidates. He said if I came out to San Diego and passed the Aviation Selection Test Battery, he'd get me a pilot slot.

That sounded great to me, so I jumped on a cross-country bus to Yuma. My mom is still mad about that. "I would have given you the money for a plane ticket!" Yeah, I know, but I wanted to do this on my own. I was an adult. I could handle it. But five days on a cross-country bus trip is quite an odyssey, with the emphasis on "odd."

## THE BUS RIDE TO YUMA

I've never seen so many Mennonites in my life. They must own stock in Greyhound. People might be on the bus for forty miles or four hundred miles. There's a lot of turnovers in the passengers.

It's hard to relax on a bus, especially for me, because I get car sick. The odors of sweat-soaked vinyl seats and gas fumes combined with the bumps on the road and other passengers who wanted to have 400-mile conversations made me want to throw up.

You just want to zone out as much as you can, but every time you're about to fall asleep, the bus makes a stop and then you have to keep your eyes open because you want to see who's getting on. I sat next to a nice old lady from Kansas for part of the trip and we had a good conversation. But at another stop some guy got on wielding a knife. They evacuated the bus when that happened.

There's a lavatory on the bus, but you want to avoid using that if you can. There were stops every couple of hours, but bus stations are always in weird, seedy parts of town. We had about half an hour to grab some fast food, use a stationary rest room, and stretch a bit. The lady from Kansas got off in Vegas, where I had my first two-dollar steak. It was my first time in Vegas, and it was pretty seedy. But Vegas and I would both grow up, and I would be back.

Shortly thereafter, I finally arrived in Yuma. After five days in the same clothes, I was feeling pretty ripe. I took a shower at my boyfriend's house, got some sleep, and then we drove to San Diego so I could take the Aviation Selection Test Battery. The Navy, Marine Corps and Coast Guard use the test to identify promising candidates for pilot training. The written test is divided into sections that evaluate cognitive ability, personality, and suitability for flight school. I felt good about how I did, but they said it would take several weeks to process the results. Then the Navy would let me know if I made the grade.

My boyfriend was headed back to North Carolina, so he gave me a ride back to New York so that I didn't have to relive the cross-country trek with unknown travel companions.

## JOB IN THE CITY

When I was back home, I took a data entry job at MacMillan Publishing. I could ride the city bus from Co-op City down to work in Lower Manhattan. The job paid $15 per hour for an eight-hour day, not including an hour for lunch. I figured if I brown-bagged it at my desk and worked during my lunch hour, I could come in at seven and go home at three, having put in a full eight hours. I did good work, but they didn't like that arrangement. I got vocal. They eventually terminated me.

Prior to my termination, I got off the bus after work one day and found my mom waiting at the stop. She wore an expression I'd never seen before. It was a mixture of happy, sad, concerned, and a few others I couldn't identify. She was holding an envelope in her hand.

"What's up?"

She handed me the envelope from the Navy, already opened. Then I understood. She was happy that I'd passed the test, concerned about what joining the military would mean for me, worried about all the unknowns, and proud that I was grown up and starting my adult life. It was a rite of passage look that every parent wears at one time or another. I'm sure I'll have plenty of those moments as a parent in the future.

But all I was thinking about when I read that letter was that I was headed for Navy officer candidate school, and I was going to earn my wings.

## Part Two
# GOLD WINGS

# THE TRANSFORMATION

THE TRANSFORMATION of civilians into military personnel must be accomplished in a matter of weeks. The metamorphosis of civilian into naval officer happens at officer candidate school (OCS). The school is designed to put you in a state of constant stress. After all, graduates in most fields, especially aviation, would be responsible for multi-million dollar equipment and lives.

This curriculum includes many of the aspects of basic training plus academic and technical courses as well as exercises to develop the skills of leadership, team building and the additional responsibilities of being a naval officer. The transition from civilian life to the military culture can be challenging, abrupt and even traumatic.

I was told to report to the Naval Aviation Medical Institute (NAMI) in Pensacola for preliminary physical tests in late April 1994. They wanted to make sure I didn't have any conditions that would prevent me from becoming an aviator. I went through several days of PT, running, swimming, and medical evaluations. During that time I met another incoming candidate named Liz Peters, a graduate of St. Louis University with a history degree.

I passed all my tests and went back home. The Navy sent a letter telling me to report to Pensacola on 11 June 1994 and check in at the Bachelor Enlisted Quarters (BEQ). I was to report to Naval Air Station Pensacola the following day after 0800 and not later than noon. So I would undergo Navy officer training at the place where I first gave serious consideration to becoming a naval aviator. When I arrived at the BEQ on the eleventh, I discovered that my roommate was Liz. We had barely gotten to know each other at NAMI, but now we acted like long-lost friends. Since Liz is the history major, I'll let her tell this story:

With all the excitement of starting the first day of OCS, we didn't sleep much. We were up early and checked out of the BEQ by nine thirty. Merryl was anxious to get started. She gave me a nudge. "What are we waiting for?" I saw there was no use killing time at the BEQ, so I agreed. We reported to NAS Pensacola at the big stone front gate and the guard pointed us toward the Regiment building, were we would be inducted.

It was June in Florida, hot and humid. Pensacola was a training center, so there were all sorts of units going through exercises– aviators, search and rescue, water survival, not to mention drills for the officer candidate classes ahead of us. They all looked serious, focused and disciplined. We wore civilian clothes and carried overnight bags. I also had a backpack with a VHS video camera and still camera. So here we were, two civilian college graduates, just strolling through the perfectly manicured grounds like tourists while future Navy leaders were put through their paces.

We found the Regiment, a long, grand, two-story building that housed the commander and staff of the OCS school, offices and classrooms, and quarters for incoming candidates during their first week. Out in front was a line of footprints painted on the pavement, each pair of footprints diverging from heel to toe at an angle of 45 degrees. We would become very familiar with these footprints during our time at OCS. Our feet would be in those footprints often.

Every Navy installation has a quarterdeck and a watch officer to greet visitors and show them where to go. We reported to this officer and he gave us the first of the endless stacks of paperwork we'd become used to in the Navy. It was only ten o'clock, and we still had two hours, but we were curious about what awaited us. We didn't have to wait long.

The nature of a candidate's induction experience is dependent on the people in charge of the induction. OCS is a twelve week program and during the first nine weeks, you're an officer candidate, and can be dismissed for any failure to meet the requirements. By the tenth week, you become a candidate officer, which means you are almost certain to graduate as long as your academics hold up and you don't sustain a serious injury. The people in charge of our induction were the candidate officers of a previous class–the last class at Pensacola that was all aviators. Subsequent classes were made up of candidates for different specialties.

The candidate officers had undergone ten weeks of intense and rigorous training at the hands of experienced drill instructors who were experts at eliminating the weak from the ranks. Like fraternity members eagerly awaiting new pledges to torment, the candidate officers were looking forward to dishing out some of the punishment they'd been taking.

As soon as they saw Merryl and me, in our civilian clothes and carrying our civilian luggage, they descended on us in a swarm, shouting orders, pointing directions, and correcting our mistakes, all at maximum volume and intensity. We were the only two members of our class to report this early, so the ratio of newly arrived civilians to candidate officers was about 1 to 12. We got the shit kicked out of us for two hours.

While we were being schooled in the ways of the Navy, the candidate officers were interrogating us. They asked Merryl, whose last name was David, "David, what do you think you're going to do in the Navy?"

"I'm going to be an aviator."

This brought various derisive responses from the aviator candidate officers, who expressed some doubt that she would succeed.

Then they asked me, "Peters, what do you think you're going to do in the Navy?"

"Aviation," I answered, and then, to my regret, added, "I think."

"You *think*? If you're not sure, what do you *really* want to do?"

"Uh, maybe supply?"

Merryl gave me a side eye glance that indicated that this was not a well-considered response. She was right. Identifying supply officer as a possible military career goal had an inflammatory effect on the candidate officers, who all converged on me. One, Andrew Davis, who was just an inch taller than I was at five foot six, got up in my face and berated me at point blank range about my indecision, my poor choice, and that the only thing lower than a supply officer was someone who aspired to be a supply officer.

So thanks to Merryl, I had two extra hours of military indoctrination, training and abuse that contributed nothing to my future effectiveness as a naval officer. I told Merryl that day, "This is two hours of my life I will never get back." Now, when I recount my service in the United States Navy, I tell people I served for 21 years, 5 months *and two hours*.

When Liz answered, "Supply officer," she drew the attention of all the other drill instructors–it was like sharks smelling blood in the water. After the feeding frenzy was over, I looked at her like, "You better keep your mouth shut." We laugh about that still.

## 8

# CHROME DOMES

THE FIRST WEEK we were housed in the Regiment building. We were issued silver helmets called "chrome domes" and olive drab utilities known as "poopy greens", because we weren't good enough to wear khakis yet. Showers were limited to three minutes. We ate in the enlisted mess since we were not fit to dine with officers or even officer candidates.

The enlisted mess had one perk - television. The only time we had access to TV was during meals, and it was tuned to a news channel. That was the week of the OJ Simpson Bronco chase on the 405 freeway, and the video was replayed day after day. So even though we had access to TV for the week, it was still mostly reruns.

After the first week, we moved into our quarters in the Battalion building, where we would spend the rest of our time at OCS. This move was known as the "bag drag," since we hauled our sea bags and other gear across the street like refugees. That's when we finally met our drill instructor. He looked like Lou Gosset from *An Officer and a Gentleman*. He had been a sniper. The officer for our class was a black female lieutenant. Liz knew her better than I did, but she wanted us both to succeed. At that time, the Navy was struggling to get minorities into aviation.

There were all sorts of corrective measures for substandard performance. They made us do lots of pushups and duck walks. If any of us did poorly in an academic exercise, the DI would yell, "Pit, get it!" That sent us to the pit, which was a big sand volleyball court. Then he supervised PT in the pit until we were covered with sand. Everywhere. Heaven forbid if you had your rifle at the time because you had to bury it in the sand, then disassemble and clean it when you were done. They wanted to break people. They wanted the quitters to quit, and the sooner the better.

A new class starts every two weeks. If you fail three tests, they roll you back into the next class, the class behind you. I told myself that I had to get through this. I can't get rolled.

We'd start the day with a mile and a half run. It was a hot, humid Florida panhandle summer. They would fly different colored flags to indicate the temperature. A black flag meant the heat and humidity were too high to run. It would be a health hazard.

In the second week, they gave us this run - six of us failed the exercise, including Liz and myself. It was way too hot and humid and we just couldn't finish. The DI called us into his office - not our regular drill instructor, but the one in charge of the run that morning. He told us that all who hadn't finished would be failed. He was going to roll back every one of us. Our jaws dropped. You could feel the tension.

This drill instructor was such a jerk, absolutely the worst. I spoke up and said, "Sir, it was a black flag when we ran it. The black flag happened as we were running the race."

I could tell he didn't believe me. It must have sounded to him like some lame excuse for failing the run, and drill instructors had heard every lame excuse in the book. He looked at me and looked at the rest of the people, then he stood up and left the office. We all just waited there, not knowing where he went or when or if he was coming back. But I didn't want to spend one extra minute at OCS, and getting rolled meant spending an extra two weeks there.

I guess the DI made some calls because he finally came back in, looking very pissed off. "Get back to class," was all he said. None of us rolled.

After we left, Liz told me, "We would have been there another two weeks if you hadn't spoken up."

## TRAINING TIME OUT

The training continued to be rigorous. One aviation student, not from our class, got so stressed out during a water exercise that he ended up drowning. To prevent that from reoccurring, they implemented a new procedure. If you were injured so seriously that continuing the exercise would result in severe bodily harm, you could yell, "Training Time Out" or just "TTO."

Our whole class was sent to the pit on one occasion. We were running in the sand. The guy in front of me injured his Achilles heel or something. He started to limp. So he yells, "Training Time Out!"

I saw the drill instructor come up to him, and he had that flat-brim campaign hat that the DI wears. The DI put the brim of his hat right up against this guy's forehead. "Did you call TTO? You fucking pussy! Don't you ever call TTO again!" This brought the kid to tears. This was a 22 year old man, in tears.

"But, my Achilles..."

"I don't give a fuck!"

I'm running by him seeing all this. For the duration of our class, nobody ever again dared to call a TTO. I'd rather die than call a TTO. I felt bad for this kid. He was a nice guy, but he got his ass chewed. It was awesome. Terrifying. It was one of those moments where you feel like you're under the greatest stress and you see something so extreme that you just laugh because it's so absurd.

We were in a classroom one hot August day when an officer candidate named Caspar was fighting a cold. While the DI was speaking, Caspar took out a handkerchief and blew his nose. It sounded like he had an amplifier in that handkerchief. The DI was pissed. He yelled at us about the proper timing and use of a handkerchief, but he didn't want anyone else to catch cold. So he closed the classroom door and cranked up the thermostat. We stayed in that sweltering room for quite some time, which did not enhance Caspar's popularity with the class.

## THE WEAK LINK

We were a bunch of young officer candidates trying to make it as a team. But women were usually assumed to be weak links, so the four women in the class got special attention. They probably saw me as a weak link because I dropped out of running all the time. I hated to run. I still do. Liz was a little heavier when we started out. She had problems running because of her weight. The drill instructors were really crappy to her. They'd call her fat and dull. One time she fell in the sand. She was covered with sweat, so the sand stuck to her. The drill instructor said, "Oh, look - a sugar cookie." They thought they could make her quit. But she sucked it up, lost twenty pounds, and kept going.

We all wanted to help each other succeed. If you were good at polishing brass, you did the brass for everybody. If you were great at polishing shoes, you were going to polish twenty pairs of shoes. But it doesn't matter how bright your brass is, how squared away your locker is, how tight your rack looks - the DI is still going to fail you, just to see how you react.

Liz got the brunt of the drill instructors' special attention. They inspected our quarters all the time. On one inspection, they failed Liz because something was out of place in her locker. Then they dumped all her stuff out of her locker onto the deck. It looked like a yard sale.

When they left, she was in tears. She completely lost it. She went on a fifteen minute rant about how she was going to quit. I sat with her and I didn't say a word. I just let her rant, watching her, with a total deadpan expression.

When she finally paused to catch her breath, I said, "Are you done?"

"Yeah, I'm done."

Then I told her, "Look, you're not going to quit. You're not going to leave me here by myself."

I'm not sure that was convincing, so I went on, "This is just a hiccup, an obstacle. We're gonna move on, we're going to go to flight school, and we're gonna freakin' crush it. Fuck this obstacle."

It took her a minute, but then she started to pick up her stuff. I helped her. She had to redo the inspection, and when she did her locker was perfect. She passed.

I couldn't let her quit. What other friend was I going to have? Most everyone else hated me. I don't think it was the color of my skin or that I was a female. I believe they just didn't like my New York attitude.

## PRESSURE TO PERFORM

For one thing, I didn't buy in to all the rah-rah stuff, "Yay, we gotta do it, we gotta fight for our country!" It's not that I didn't care about that. There were some times I felt very patriotic, and times I enjoyed the camaraderie. But to me, OCS was a hurdle to get over. I didn't need to go to a pep rally every day, especially as the pressure was building to perform.

By the tenth week, we were doing a series of PT tests as a class. It was very competitive. We had a guidon, a flag that one candidate officer carries to identify your class. As you win each competition, you get a streamer for your flag, and the more streamers, the better chance you have of becoming an honor class. We were doing the drill portion and everyone was nervous, everyone was pumped. The rest of the class was jumping up and down like a football team before the kickoff of the big game. "We're gonna do it!" There was lots of adrenaline and excitement.

I was motivated and, as you know by now, I'm highly competitive. But when I'm under stress I become centered, quiet and focused. I don't show emotion. I might run the scenario over and over in my head, planning how to overcome the obstacle, considering different paths to take. The class leader thought I was being an ass because I wasn't all pumped up like everyone else. He was yelling at me, trying to get me to show team spirit by using up a lot of energy that I was planning to put to better use in the competition. He was doing all the talking, really pushing it. Finally I said, "Bro, get outa my face or I'm gonna friggin' put my paws on you." He backed off.

We won that particular competition. I was happy about it. When they put that streamer on the guidon, you could feel the emotion. We were almost crying like kids because we got the streamer after ten weeks of sweat and tears. Inside, I was strutting with pride, but outside I was deadpan. If I was a computer, you'd think somebody hit my ALT CTL DEL buttons. I was like a duck on water, looking cool on the surface, but down below I'm paddling like hell, scared that an alligator is going to come and kill me. That's how I roll.

I was determined to succeed and I wasn't going to allow any obstacle or distraction to get in my way, whether it was the mile swim, the dunker tank, or the obstacle course. Any candidate who failed to complete OCS automatically entered the Navy as an enlisted person, assigned to a billet of the Navy's choosing. There was no flying for people who failed or dropped out. I could not allow myself to fail.

## ATTITUDE

*When you lose focus, you pay a price.*

Everybody in the class had a call sign. Like a nickname, you don't choose your own. It is bestowed by the drill instructors early in the process. You get a shirt with your call sign on it and you wear it during PT. Call signs were usually not complimentary. My call sign was "Attitude." I think it was because I didn't like to run and the drill instructor was mad at me. But it could have been a lot of other things, too.

We graduated on time in September. Out of an original class of 37, we lost four or five. Out of four females who started, three finished—myself, Liz and a woman who was going to be a Seabee, a Navy combat engineer. We came out as Navy ensigns, the lowest officer rank, but still officers.

## WE GIVE HER OUR ALL, SHE GIVES US HER COLORS

Liz graduated to flight school, but she got medically disqualified. She blew out her ear drums. It was probably better because she really did want to be a supply officer. And you know, she was an exceptional supply officer. She was a rocket in her field and had a great career.

Our class had a commemorative t-shirt made with all sorts of Navy icons and images that were important to our class. Prominent was a drill instructor's face in front of a big American flag. Our class motto was at the bottom: "We give her our all, she gives us her colors."

I came out of OCS with more genuine patriotic feeling than I'd had when I started. It's not that I didn't love my country before, but when you accept the responsibility to fight for the United States and know you may be called upon to give up your life for the freedoms we all enjoy, patriotism becomes real. That's why I would never disrespect our flag. I've folded too many flags, seen too many people sacrificing to serve, heard too many stories about what our POWs had to go through. Even if I hadn't become a pilot, I would still have served, because our freedom is sacred to me.

OCS was a challenge, and I always enjoy a challenge. But, if you offered me two million dollars to do it again, I'd say, "No way."

# FLYING SOLO

*Fear of failure is the precursor to something great.*

Up until World War II, all naval aviators did their primary training at Pensacola. But the war effort required more Navy fliers, so additional training centers were established. Texas congressman Lyndon Johnson got one for his home state to be located near the Gulf coast town of Corpus Christi. That is where I took my first flight as a student naval aviator.

I arrived at NAS Corpus Christi in March 1995. My first instructor was named Hernandez. He was tall, lanky, and about to separate from the Navy. He was a good guy.

My first flight was in a T-34, a two-seat, single-engine, prop-driven trainer made my Beechcraft. The Navy had been teaching students to fly in T-34s since the 1940s.

I went out to the flight line and did the walk around. I felt pretty confident. I wasn't all excited, thinking, "I'm accomplishing my dreams!" I was focused on procedures, on getting the check list right. I was looking for anything that wasn't right, thinking about the systems. "Let's survive this. Let's show the instructor I'm good and I've got what it takes." I don't think of how much fun it is until after the flight. If I'm enjoying the flight, there's one part of me that's thinking, "This is too much fun. What am I missing?"

Air sickness was common during the first training flight, and it was not unusual for a student to throw up in the cockpit. Being forewarned, I knew I didn't want to get sick and go through dry heaves, so I fortified myself with a greasy hamburger at lunch.

In March it was already like summer on the coast, and hotter on the pavement, so you're already dripping as you walk out to the flight line. Every orifice is sweaty, you can feel perspiration dripping down your back, like when you're working out. Once you get in and close the canopy, which is sometimes called a "greenhouse" for good reason, the temperature goes up very quickly. The instructor didn't even get in until I had finished the check list–that's how hot it was.

Hernandez taxied out. For some people the first experience of flying is not comfortable. You're taxiing, it's hot, you're strapped into a parachute, flight suit, helmet, O2 mask. I am prone to car sickness, and taxiing with the canopy open and all that hot engine exhaust washing over me brought on a queasy feeling. The presence of a barf bag in the cockpit did not reassure me.

Fortunately, I did not need the barf bag on that flight or any other in my career. But later, when I became an instructor, I had students throw up in the cockpit. It's gross because even as the instructor in the back seat, you can still smell it. One time I got mad at a student because he had a ham and cheese sandwich before the flight. You're not supposed to have a heavy meal, especially if you are prone to airsickness. So I was pissed off. "You will not ever eat ham and cheese when you fly with me! You eat saltine crackers and nothing else!" It was so nasty.

As we took off over the Gulf of Mexico, Hernandez pointed out all the reference points for takeoffs and landings. This was before

GPS, so all you had was a map and visual reference points. "You want to be at 3000 feet when you cross Padre Island, 1500 feet when you're even with that radio tower," stuff like that. The student just sits back and observes the cadence of the flight. There were eight separate boxes of air space for training flights so that student pilots didn't run into each other. The instructor told you where the boundaries were. For the student it was a sight-seeing flight, but you had to remember the sights because you were going to use every one of them. It was like learning the underground mazes at Co-op City.

If the instructor felt comfortable and the student wasn't throwing up, he'd say, "You wanna fly for a little bit?"

"Yeah, I wanna fly." He gave me the controls and I got the feel of the T-34. I learned how to use the trim wheels. The T-34 is pretty stable. Once you get it trimmed up, you can take your hands off and she'll fly straight. At least, she'll fly straight if the student doesn't have a death grip on the stick, overcorrecting for every deviation.

When you're first flying, you're white knuckling the stick, fighting the control forces. If it's trimmed right, you don't have to do that. But if it's not trimmed right, and the instructor says, "Take your hands off," then the aircraft goes into a climb or dive. That means you did it wrong. It's okay if it happens. That's how you learn.

As the student gets more experience flying, the instructor will take the controls, intentionally take the aircraft out of trim, and then hand the controls back to the student. Then you have to work the trim wheels very quickly to restore the aircraft's trim because the instructor will be counting down. "Five, four, three, two, HANDS OFF!" The student releases the controls and the aircraft had better be properly trimmed because if it doesn't fly straight and level with your hands off the controls, you have failed to impress the instructor.

• • •

That was for later. On our first flight, I was just taking it all in, feeling the airplane under my control, getting the feel of the T-34. The flight was almost over. Hernandez asked, "Anything else you want to see?"

Most students, if they're not nauseous during that first flight, ask to see a loop or an aileron roll. But I knew what I wanted. "I want to be in inverted flight."

"Really?" I could hear the sigh in his voice. It's a lot of extra work. He went through his checklist. One limiting factor for inverted flight in the T-34 is that all the oil goes into the sump and doesn't circulate, so you can't keep that up for long or you jack up the engine. "Okay, but we're only going to do this for a maximum of thirty seconds."

He was working hard to maintain inverted flight. If I had known more, I'd have asked to depart from controlled flight and just let the aircraft fall out of the sky. But I didn't have the experience to ask for that. Flying inverted, it's like some one pushing your gut in. It takes a moment to get used to it. Also, all the crap on the floor of the cockpit falls down onto the canopy, like somebody emptied a vacuum cleaner in the cockpit.

## GRAMPS

Hernandez separated early in training, so I got a new "onwing," which was my primary instructor. Students train with several instructors, but your "onwing" is the one you spend most of your time with, the one who knows you best. He was Lt. Ronnie Robinson, a white Southern gentleman with absolutely white hair. We called him "Gramps," but not to his face. His corrections of student mistakes in the air were immediate, emphatic and delivered at maximum volume. He pretty much yelled at me the whole time. Ronnie Robinson was not as easy going as Hernandez. He was a demanding instructor.

·  ·  ·

On the ground, preparing for a training flight, Gramps would speak in a calm, mild tone, letting me know what to expect in the upcoming exercise and also how he would evaluate me. It was very reassuring.

But as soon as I strapped into my seat, with Gramps in the seat behind me, it was like a switch was thrown and this kindly Southern gentleman turned into a stern taskmaster. "Why are you doing this? Why are you doing that?" He was on me about every thing I did, and we hadn't even left the ground. Once in the air, he didn't let up.

If I was setting up for an emergency landing and did anything that was not correct, he'd curse me out. I'd get all flustered. "I told you to do it this way–do it again!" Then he'd abruptly take control of the aircraft, swing us around in a tight circle, and set us up again for another try.

One time the storm of profanity in my headphones was so withering, I put my head down in the cockpit, thinking, "Oh my God, I'm failing this ride."

"What the fuck are you doing with your head down? You can't see a goddamn thing down there!" This was followed by a barrage of all the ways I sucked at being a pilot. I really contemplated opening the canopy and bailing out of that aircraft.

Then we'd land and he would calmly say, "Well that was an average flight." He wasn't hard to please - he just wanted perfection. Sometimes on the ground we joked around a little, but in the air he mostly rode my ass. I would dream about being in that aircraft. I would fly training missions in my dreams, so there was no escape even in my sleep. It was a very stressful experience, but when it came time for my check ride, I had a two point above average score, which was very rare. Gramps' methods worked. They were a great peril to my sanity, but they worked.

The day of my solo finally came. I was confident in my skills and was looking forward to clearing the next milestone. But then I got into the airplane and took off. That's when I got nervous. I could sense something was wrong, something was missing. Everything looked normal, conditions were good, the airplane was performing just as it should. The engine sounded smooth, but louder than usual. There were other noises I hadn't heard before - control cables flexing, control surfaces moving, the air flow changing in volume and tone. Finally, it hit me. I was hearing these noises for the first time because Gramps wasn't in the back seat yelling at me. His comments, corrections and condemnations had been so loud and constant that I hadn't heard all those sounds that the T-34 makes in flight. Once I realized that it was the voice of experience that was missing, the solo proceeded smoothly to a successful conclusion.

## FORMATION FLYING

After the student solos, learns aerobatics, solos again, and learns instrument flying, the last step in training is formation flying. Students are paired up so that they learn to read each other and predict each other's moves. You are connected at the hip for a few weeks, and you learn to fly formation with one another. I was paired up with another New Yorker whose call sign was "Rock." I don't know why, maybe he had rocks for hands, maybe that was his call sign before. We started working with each other. First, we'd walk around the hangar in formation. We called ourselves Big Apple flight because we're from New York. We communicated as if we were flying in formation. There's a lead and a wing man. "Big Apple, lining up, ready for takeoff," we'd say to each other, as if in radio communication while flying. "Okay, I'm gonna break away. One, two, three - break."

The way the lead flies dictates the way the wing man flies. You have to trust the other pilot to be there when he's supposed to be there and do what he's supposed to do. The lead has to be predictable because unpredictable maneuvers end badly. It was the first time I had to trust another person to that extent. We did well. When the lead rocked his wings to the left, I knew he was going to bank left, so I started my left turn as well. If he screwed up, if he rocked left and then didn't go left, he had to get on the radio immediately and say, "No, I screwed up, I meant right." The lead has to be predictable and the wing man has to be aggressive to stay in position to maintain the integrity of the flight. It's almost like a dance.

As lead you have to have a very stable platform. Your air work can't be sloppy. You can't be going up and down in altitude because then your wing man is all over the place. When you look at a formation in flight, it looks smooth, precise. But the wing men are working their asses off, doing small corrections the whole time. It's like a whip. Every deviation of the lead is magnified by the wing man trying to match it. You have to trust that the lead is going to be stable.

## TOP GUN STYLE

At the conclusion of primary flight training at Corpus Christi, students were evaluated by instructors for one of four assignments - jets, helicopters, E2C2 or props. Everybody wants jets because that's the Top Gun stuff, operating jet fighters and bombers from aircraft carriers. And jet pilots had the best chance of becoming Navy test pilots, and test pilots had the best chance of becoming astronauts.

You could indicate a preference for any of the classifications, but you needed a minimum score of 50 on the Navy Standard Score to qualify for jets. Gramps, my onwing, was trying to talk me into E2C2s, twin prop early warning aircraft, because they operate from carriers, and I would get my catapult qualification. I left jets as my first choice, then E2C2, then helos, and put props last.

Then I thought about what the San Diego recruiter had told me - that the Navy was motivated to get more minorities into naval aviation. I wondered, if I made it, would my advanced instructors look at me and think the only reason I was there is because I'm a black female, and there's a quota.

I didn't need to worry. I got 49.1 on the Navy Standard Score, nine tenths of a point too low for jets. I got my third choice, helicopters. I wouldn't get catapult qualified, but helicopters have offensive weapons and E2C2s were unarmed.

## BE SO GOOD, THEY CAN'T DISMISS YOU

Missing the cut-off by such a narrow margin made me wonder why. Was I really not good enough? Was there resentment among instructors against the emphasis on minority students? Was it my attitude?

I talked to Gramps about my score. Our instructor-student relationship was over. We were now just two Navy officers, one with much greater experience. He told me that one of his classmates in flight school was a black officer. They got to be good friends going through the program.

He said, "Merryl, let me tell you something. When you're in the military a lot of people are going to think a lot of things when they see you. They're going to think you're probably not supposed to be there, for one reason or another. You're one of the best student pilots I've ever flown with. Without a doubt. Hands down. There's going to be a point where you perform and continue to perform and perform so well that they're going to run out of excuses of why you're there and just accept the fact that you're good at what you do."

I took his words to heart. There are people who are going to think all kinds of things about you, that you're inferior, that you don't belong on the streets of your own neighborhood. You just have to perform and let your actions speak for themselves. I never stopped giving it my all because I wouldn't allow myself to fail.

Now when I speak to high school students, I tell them the same thing. You have to perform at the highest level. If your friends are dealing drugs, you cannot be hanging out with them because you'll be guilty by association. You have to separate yourself from that. I understand the pressures of being in the city and hanging with your friends. When I was in college I had to walk away from my friends who smoked weed. I knew I could not be associated with that. You'll have friends who want to party and you'll want you to go to the party. You have to say no. You gotta stay your ass home and study. The long-term goal is much more important than one night of fun.

You must commit to a goal. You can't say, "I'll do it tomorrow." You gotta do it at that moment. If you continue to perform at a high level they will have to admit you're good. If they don't, they're in denial. Like Jay-Z says, it's just dirt on your shoulder. That's what they are. They're just dirt. Brush it off. People will tell me it's easy for me to say that. Bro, I lived it.

Be so good, they can't dismiss you. Some wise white dude told me that. You want to bash white males, go ahead. But when a white male who knows the system and knows the other side gives you advice like that, I listen. Especially when it comes from some one who rode my ass and flew with me for months. He expected nothing less than perfection from me and I gave it to him. You gotta respect that.

# 10

# CHANCE ENCOUNTERS

*I may be an asshole but, I am an asshole with a heart.*

FROM CORPUS CHRISTI, it was back to Pensacola to learn to fly helicopters. Transitioning from linear flight to helicopters was an adjustment. Learning the aerodynamics and ground work wasn't bad, but the first training flight was frustrating.

Our training aircraft was the TH-57, military version of the Bell Jet Ranger. My instructor took me out to the middle of a field where there was a big white square painted on the ground with an H in the middle of it. He hovered over the H. The two main controls in a helicopter are the cyclic, which is like the stick in an airplane, and the collective, which controls power. He had one finger on the cyclic, and the helicopter was in a stable hover.

"Okay, you got the aircraft," he said. And now I had the controls. For a split second, everything was fine, then the aircraft started to deviate and naturally I tried to correct. It felt like I had meathooks for hands–every control input was magnified and it was a mess. When you have control input on a helicopter, there's always a delay before the aircraft reacts, so there is a tendency to have more control input than is necessary. It took four or five flights to learn to hover. Then we learned about autorotation, what happens when you lose an engine, and all the other cool stuff you can do in a helicopter.

I've never had to eject or bale out of an aircraft, but the Navy prepares you for that eventuality - sort of. Ejecting and parachuting are both dangerous, and by the time an aviator gets to advanced training, she is too valuable an asset to risk in those hazardous exercises. So in Pensacola, part of pre-flight training was parachute training. We went through the basics, jumping off a little platform, learning how to land and roll so that we don't break our legs or our knees. A lot of people get hurt even in this stage. We never actually used a parachute, but they did take us parasailing. They took us out until we reached a certain altitude over the water in our parasails, and then they'd cut the line. We'd drift down into the water and then our job was to unclip from the apparatus and stay afloat until they came and pulled us out of the water.

Helicopter training included instrument flying, which means you trust the instruments to tell you the status of your aircraft even when meteorological conditions limit visibility. The instructor would take up two students at a time, one to fly and the other to observe from the rear seat. The instructor would do things like pull a circuit breaker to see if the student would notice and react properly. Of course, the observer was not allowed to tell the other student, "Hey, he just pulled a circuit breaker." So when I was the observer and saw the instructor try something, I'd squeeze the harness of the student to let him know to be on his toes.

## CROSS COUNTRY

Once the student has advanced in training, she does cross-country flights with an instructor and another student. One weekend we went to Key West in the TH-57. It was so slow, we could barely keep up with traffic on I95. But once we got to Key West, we went snorkelling, hit some of the bars, did the whole tourist thing.

I had another flight with Rock, my formation partner from Corpus Christi, who was now also training in HT 18. By now we had been training together so long, we were like brother and sister. It was supposed to be an out-and-back from Pensacola to Panama City, a round trip that would be completed during the day. But the weather came in faster than expected and we were stuck. There were no military quarters for us in Panama City, and we hadn't brought any clothes for an overnight stay. We were two young ensigns, cash-strapped and stranded.

There was no other choice than to stay in a hotel, but the budget was tight. We rented one room with two beds. I told Rock, "We will not tell anyone we did this." By this time we were like brother and sister. But we were like a brother and sister from New York City, so after we checked in, we went out on the town in Panama City and partied it up. There was no use letting bad weather ruin the whole evening.

## YOU HAD ME AT HELO

People ask which I like better - helicopters or fixed wing aircraft. It's apples and oranges. You can pull 7g turns in a fixed wing, something you can't do in a helo. Fixed wing aircraft can be beautiful. We used to say the reason helicopters fly is that they're so ugly, the earth repels them. But helicopters are exciting and fun. It's tactical flying, close to the ground, zipping around. Flying backwards, stopping and hovering, you realize military aircraft are just cool period. It's sexy because it's a lot of stick and rudder. A plane, you fly forward, you turn. In a helo, you can stop on a dime, pivot, and keep flying. Maneuverability is so fun, you can finesse it, fly the hell out of it. You can be as aggressive as you want.

•  •  •

I ranked number two in my class, so I was likely to get my first choice, the SH60B. It was the newest Navy helicopter at the time and it carried anti-submarine and air-to-surface weapons. I also thought there was a good chance I'd be based on the East Coast, so I'd be close to my mom.

## GOLDEN GRADUATION

Mom came down for graduation in August 1996, as did my godmother, and Liz. Pinning on the gold wings of a naval aviator is a proud rite of passage. There was a tradition in which a colleague pins the wings to the newly minted naval aviator by punching the pins through the aviator's garment and into her flesh. This was known as "blood wings," and the practice had recently been prohibited. Liz was on stage to pin on my wings. Evidently, she was not aware of the new regulations, because when she pinned on my wings, she gave them the traditional punch.

I thought about where I'd come from and the journey I'd taken to earn those wings. There was pain all along the way because of who I was, where I was going, and what it took to get there. Nothing worthwhile is attained without pain, and getting those wings was worth every bit of it. Those wings were there to stay.

Later, we all went out to celebrate - new aviators, family, and friends. It got pretty wild. It was the first time my mom partied with my Navy buddies, and they loved her. It was also the first time I remember seeing my mom let her hair down and enjoy herself. Maybe it was because she now knew her daughter was going places. I guess she had a couple of drinks, because at one point I turned around and one of my instructors was reclining in my mom's lap and his nose was in her boobs. She was holding him like a baby. What the hell was happening in this alternate universe? The wheels were clearly coming off the bus. We all had a great time.

## SURVIVOR

I was assigned to SH60Bs and went for training in that aircraft to Naval Station Mayport, near Jacksonville, Florida. My training squadron was HSL40. HSL stood for Helicopter, anti-Submarine, Light. The first part of training is the pilot phase where you learn to fly the aircraft. But before you do that, you have to learn the systems - electrical, environmental, oil, fuel, hydraulics, even the brake system. You learn emergency procedures and the performance envelope.

Before I could proceed to the second half of training, somebody got the bright idea to send me to SERE school. SERE stands for Survival, Evasion, Resistance, and Escape. It was designed to teach vital survival skills to people operating in environments where capture by the enemy is a possibility. This course teaches you how to sustain yourself if your airplane goes down in enemy territory. You learn how to evade your captors, how to resist your captors if you are caught and coerced to talk, and then how to escape from your captors. As you can see, most of those elements deal with the subject of capture, so it seemed that capture was a foregone conclusion.

It was January when I arrived in Brunswick, Maine, for SERE school. January is cold in most of the northern hemisphere, but particularly so in Maine. We started out with classroom work, but then it was time to put that knowledge to use in the field.

They assigned us partners. Mine was a nice white guy. They dropped off the two-person teams in different parts of the remote wilderness. The ostensible objective was to hike out to safety, but the snow was eight feet deep, so hiking seemed optimistic. Fortunately, the snow was also deep enough to build a snow cave, and that was our shelter.

In 1995, the Navy was just getting used to integrating females into the ranks, and they weren't fully prepared. One indication of this was that GI footwear was mostly in larger, men's sizes. The boots I had were a little big. This was a tactical error on my part. Ordinarily this would not have been a problem, but on a winter survival course, small problems tend to become larger problems. In the two days we were in the elements, my feet were getting cold. Snow would get inside my boot, then melt, then freeze. It became increasingly difficult to walk, so it was hard to evade successfully.

Experienced military personnel played the part of the enemy, searching for us and tracking us down. This was a familiar environment to them, so it was their home turf. Also, it wasn't hard to follow the footprints of two people lost in the snow. We were captured relatively early, on the second day. This was fortunate because by then I couldn't feel my right foot. I took off my gloves and my fingertips were white and waxy.

The exercise doesn't end when you get captured. You are treated as a prisoner would be treated by an enemy. Most of the details of this training are classified, but we were taken to our enclosures which represented the lodgings we might expect an enemy to furnish us with. By that time, my foot began to thaw and I've never felt such agonizing pain in my life. It's not like going out in the snow and getting cold, then coming back and sitting in front of the fire to get that pins and needles feeling. This was searing pain, and not just in my feet, but throughout my whole body. It was so severe that my vision blurred, but I didn't know whether the cause was frostbite, hunger, stress or something else. My captors knew about my condition because they were examining my foot regularly.

Now would have been an understandable time to call a Training Time Out, but I remembered what happened to that guy in OCS when he called a TTO. I would be taken out of the SERE course and I would have to repeat it. I could be left behind. So, despite the pain, I didn't call a TTO. I didn't complain about the pain.

They kept me in the course, which is to say I remained a prisoner and they continued the training.

They tried to warm my feet up. That was even more painful. I'd rather try to knock down a brick wall with my bare head than go through that pain again. I lost track of time. After about twelve hours they gave me a Percocet. I could not walk. When my captors wanted to question me, they had to send two guys in to pick me up and carry me.

I said, "Thank you so much for carrying me around everywhere." They just rolled their eyes and carried my limp ass everywhere I had to go. I thought it was funny, but the excruciating pain took away a lot of the humor.

I still had to follow the resistance protocols correctly to pass the course, especially during the "interviews." Most of the protocols are about not cooperating with the enemy, withholding information, and, least likely in my case, trying to escape. I don't know how I was able to focus and resist. All I knew was that I didn't want to spend one extra minute in this course, and that meant I had to hold it together until the end. I later found out during debrief that I did pretty well during this part of the training.

Finally, they blindfolded me and took me to the hospital. I would have just kept going even though, now that I think about it, that was crazy. I was determined to get through the training. No one is asking you, "Do you want to quit?" And I wasn't going to ask. No way.

The only fear I had was due to the pain. I wasn't sure what my medical condition was.

## CLOSE TO KILLING A UNICORN

In the hospital they put me on a morphine drip. I'm not going to lie; having a doctor prescribe morphine is glorious. The nurses were wonderful. One asked, "Is there anything you want?" And I said, in my morphine-induced state, "Can I have some pancakes please? And some oranges?" Then I must have remembered I was in Maine, because I also asked for lobster. I'm a big lobster fan and I hadn't eaten much for two days.

I stayed in the hospital another day while they assessed my condition. While I was there, the commander of the SERE school and his executive officer came in and asked how I was doing. I didn't think this was standard procedure, but then I found out that of the 32 people in the SERE class, 28 were suffering from frostbite. The SERE school command probably got their asses chewed for that. There were very few black and even fewer black female aviators at the time. They came close to killing a unicorn.

I was still in a lot of pain. I was on crutches for another six weeks. All my fingertips were frostbitten except for my right pinkie. Half of my right foot was frostbitten. It swelled to twice its normal size, and my skin had a wax candle appearance. They wrapped me up and applied lots of silver Sulfadiazine cream on the extremities. I did physical therapy for several weeks, putting my foot in a whirlpool twice a week to keep the circulation going so my foot would not die. But those hospital nurses - they brought me lobster.

## COLD WAR ENEMY

In 2004, I went through additional advanced training beyond the SERE course. By then we were at war in the Persian Gulf and the Middle East. The environment had changed. We would be flying in areas where the enemy reacted differently than a potential Cold War enemy. If you are a pilot in the Middle East and you get captured, the odds of living are going to be pretty low. The odds of being beheaded with a sword are much higher.

What happens in the advanced course is also classified. I can say that it was intense, and not only in a physical way, but mentally as well. During my original SERE training, I learned the "tap code," which allowed prisoners to communicate with each other even when housed in separate cells. It was developed by an F-105 pilot shot down over North Vietnam in 1965. He spent eight years in the Hanoi Hilton, which is what our guys called the North Vietnamese POW camp in Hanoi. That officer's name was Smitty Harris. I had the pleasure of meeting him years later at a Gathering of Eagles event. He was really a cool dude. It's great to know him.

Because of my SERE experience, I was rolled back into the next class, so I was delayed in starting the tactical phase of training at HSL40. In this section of the program, you learn to employ the aircraft as a weapon system. The SH60B can carry torpedoes, sonobuoys, Hellfire and Penguin missiles as well as a FLIR system used to laser-mark targets for other air or surface forces. The SH60B is also used in search and rescue applications, passenger and cargo transport and as a communication link. We learned how these systems worked and what types of targets they could be used against.

Most pilots strive to learn as much about the aircraft as possible. The more you know, the less surprised you will be when something goes wrong. If you know the systems and know the aircraft, you can analyze the problem and take the appropriate action. To have complete understanding of the aircraft and weapons deployment makes you much more lethal in how you do things. It also earns respect from your peers. It gives you street cred.

## THE DATING SCENE

By this time I had broken up with my boyfriend from North Carolina. I was checking out Internet Relay Chat and ended up in a chat room called "Hot Tub." There were people who were fun to talk to. This one guy was interesting. He was attending the University of Arkansas, studying physics. He had an unusual name - Kjell, pronounced like "cello" without the "o."

It's Norwegian. We talked in the chat room, then more on the phone. I could tell by his voice he was kind of nerdy, somebody who would understand a girl from the Island of Misfit Toys. He sounded kind and intelligent. He was someone I connected with.

We exchanged pictures via computer. His looked okay. The one I sent him was of me and my ex-boyfriend. He said, "Your picture looks good, but it would be better without that other guy in it."

Finally I suggested he come out for spring break and we could hang out a little bit. He thought that was a good idea. So I asked him, "What are you driving?"

"A van."

"Dude, if you don't have a Great Dane and a bunch of teenagers, you shouldn't have a van."

"It's a custom van."

"That doesn't make it better."

But he came anyway and we hung out. We started dating. I had no idea this would be my future husband. Kjell says if we had passed each other on the street, neither of us would have noticed the other. But we connected, just before my first long cruise deployment at sea.

# 11

# ON THE GOOD SHIP

In September 1997, I transferred to HSL 48, an operational SH60B squadron. The squadron was split into detachments. My detachment, which included two aircraft, three helicopter aircraft commanders (HAC), three helicopter second pilots (H2P), two air crewmen and almost twenty maintenance personnel, was assigned to the cruiser *Normandy*, CG-60. We would be part of a battle group built around the aircraft carrier *George Washington*. On the upcoming deployment to the Mediterranean, *Normandy* would be the shotgun cruiser. Her primary mission was to stay close to the carrier and interdict incoming threats.

There was a month of work-up cruises off the East Coast to get everybody used to working together. The Navy was still in the process of integrating women in combat roles. *Normandy* had four females out of a crew of about 400. We had a four-rack cabin and our own washroom, and we got a lot of attention.

There's usually some good-natured rivalry between aviation personnel and the ship's company. I have the utmost respect for ships' company because they work hard. Everybody on the ship stands watches except for the aviation detachment. We take up space, we eat their food, but we basically have no responsibilities beyond flying and taking care of the helos. Surface warfare crews call us "Airedales," not always a term of esteem. We call them "shoes," from the tradition of aviation personnel wearing brown shoes and surface warfare people wearing black shoes. The name for a non-aviation naval person was shortened to "shoe," which we jokingly said was an acronym for "stupidest human on earth."

The highest ranking officers in the aviation detachment were the Officer in Charge (OIC), the Maintenance Officer and the Operations Officer. These three officers were also the HACs. We pilots who had just graduated from SH60B school were the H2Ps on all flights. Rock was also an H2P in our detachment.

Two of our HACs were good. The third was not. He was our operations officer, a weak pilot who was also weak as an aircraft commander. He lacked decision making skills and he was also a jerk. He came close to killing me, himself and an air crewman.

I had graduated at the top of my class and I had strong skills and technical knowledge. On one particular night, the air crewman in the back was experienced, a rescue swimmer and competent. The operations officer was our HAC. It was three in the morning and we were half way through a seven-hour anti-submarine scenario. There was no moon and it was hazy. The sky and sea were just black and you couldn't see any difference between them.

We were hunting a sub. We could use electronic equipment to track it and locate it, but obviously we were not going to deploy any weapons because the submarine was one of ours, playing the role of an intruder. We would win the scenario by visually identifying the sub–one of us had to see it.

Our air crewman had done a good job of tracking with the sonobuoy. He had us hovering right over the sub which was submerged just below the surface. But looking down all any of us could see was the black of the water. We knew the submarine was below us, but we couldn't score a "kill" unless one of us saw it. Our crewman was standing in the open hatch, leaning out over the water and peering down into the impenetrable darkness.

We were hovering at 200 feet because that was the minimum altitude allowed during a night time scenario. A month before, a helo crew was flying at low level at night, the pilot wasn't paying attention, and he baptized a perfectly good SH60B. They all survived, miraculously, to brief us about what happens when you fly too low above the ocean at night. Their mishap resulted in restricting night flying to a minimum altitude of 200 feet.

But there was a loophole in the new regs. We were allowed to descend to 50 feet in coupled flight, meaning if we were on autopilot. And the coupled flight rules didn't specify day or night, so there was some ambiguity in the regulations. And we certainly couldn't see the sub from 200 feet up on a completely dark night. The HAC explained his interpretation of the regs and said, "Let's just go down to 50 feet in coupled flight. Then we'll drop a flare and we'll be able to see the sub."

Being young and stupid, I said, "Okay."

He asked me to take out the check list for low level coupled approach at night. Even on autopilot with very precise instruments, fifty feet is a dangerous altitude at night. I can't remember what the sea state was, probably because I couldn't see it in the dark, but at fifty feet a big wave could come dangerously close to slapping us out of the sky.

Poring over the manual, I furiously searched for the procedural checklist. I'm new, it's night time, it's hard to see. I'm fumbling through pages, but I can't find the checklist. My head is buried in the cockpit. I knew the procedure, but the HAC wanted to go through the checklist. That was exactly the way it should have been done.

But, unbeknownst to me, the pilot had already departed from coupled flight and was controlling the aircraft manually, in violation of the new regulations. He was descending below 200 feet even though we could not see the surface of the water or visually determine how high we were above it, just as we were advised not to do by the crew that went in the very same way.

It's very difficult to tell in a helicopter to detect vertical or horizontal motion if you have no visual reference points. But that's not a problem because you have precise instruments that tell you how high you are. Unfortunately, since I was searching through the manual, I was not looking at the instruments. I assumed the command pilot was. Never assume.

"Did you find it?" he asked, a question which I also assumed meant that he had not started his descent because he was waiting for the check list.

"Still looking." I was frustrated and feeling stupid. Why couldn't I find it?

All of a sudden I felt the aircraft kind of bump. I'm still not sure what caused that. I looked up at the altimeter because that's always the first instrument you look at. It showed that we were in a rapid descent and we were already below twenty feet.

"Power!" Even as I yelled it, I was grabbing a whole armpit full of collective because there was no time to wait for the HAC to respond. That halted our descent and the crewman in the back said that at that moment he finally saw the surface of the ocean and it was about six feet below the aircraft. We would definitely have hit the water if I hadn't acted.

We gained altitude and returned to the ship in total silence. No one said anything. We had been ordered not to descend below 200 feet, and not below 50 in coupled flight. This jackass did a manual descent below 20 feet in pitch blackness because he got disoriented or distracted and I was too busy looking for the checklist.

When a helicopter goes into the water, the rotor blades cause it to flip over as it sinks. My crewman would have been fucked. I don't think any of us would have gotten out.

. . .

Back on *Normandy*, we still didn't talk, didn't say a word, didn't even debrief. We just went to bed. We never mentioned it again. I don't know why. Maybe we didn't want an investigation, maybe I was embarrassed that I hadn't got through the check list fast enough, or maybe we'd all just come too close to a cold, wet burial at sea. There were no consequences. I had to fly with that pilot over the next six months during the regular rotation during our deployment, but I never trusted him and never took my eyes off the windscreen or the instruments while he was flying.

I learned a lot from that incident. Pilots and crew have to communicate effectively throughout the mission. They call it cockpit resource management, CRM. I can't assume I know what anyone else in the aircraft is doing, and I can't assume that they know what I'm doing. We have to talk. Above all, never blindly place your faith in the person with the most experience. No one, no matter how many hours he has, is infallible. We almost paid a high price to learn those lessons.

## DEPLOYMENT

Our deployment with the battle group was supposed to be five months in the Mediterranean followed by a month in the Persian Gulf, then back home. Our first port visit was Greece, but after that we were redirected because Saddam Hussein wouldn't sign an agreement called The Iraqi Liberation Act. He had a deadline and the battle group was supposed to launch missiles if he didn't sign. So we spent the rest of our time in the Gulf. We did recon, checked certain areas for smuggling activity, observed Iranian ships and "fishing vessels." We'd be out to sea for thirty days, in port for three to replenish, then out again.

Kjell and I were staying in touch. We had e-mail, but at that time all e-mail messages, incoming and outgoing, had to be cleared through an officer in the ship's company. There were no private e-mails. So Kjell and I sent cassette tapes back and forth, which were not censored. And we wrote real letters, on paper.

I became friends with a lieutenant from the ship's company named Tom. He was distraught, going through a divorce. We were buddies. Ashore, we would get up early, run three miles, and at night we'd check out the local scene and party.

On the ship, we'd just hang out. Sometimes we'd be in his cabin, talking about his life, his marriage falling apart, private stuff. We'd close the door, but then the rumors really started to fly. Believe it or not, every female does not want to sleep with every male on the ship. Men and women can maintain a professional relationship. But as a woman, I had to expect greater scrutiny, fair or not. And I was definitely being scrutinized.

By the third or fourth month of what was supposed to be a six month cruise, but now might be extended, people were tired and worn out. Things that were fun in the beginning lost their appeal. People you could tolerate at the start of the cruise were getting on your nerves. And when false rumors made the rounds and I got the looks and heard the nasty comments, and it never ceased, I just wanted to go home.

One day I was on the flight deck, breaking down in tears. Why was I being judged by these people? If we had been two guys, this wouldn't be happening. The OIC of our aviation detachment, Lt. Commander Blaisdell, came up. He was soft-spoken, but carried a lot of authority - a good officer.

"Hey Merryl, what's up?" Then he saw the condition I was in. "What's wrong?"

I said I was tired of being on the boat because everybody thinks I'm sleeping with this officer and it's not true. He's going through a tough time and I'm just trying to be a friend. I was sick of it.

He listened as I poured out my long, sad tale. Then he said, "Okay, I got it."

I don't know what he said or whom he said it to, but after that, people left us alone. I don't know if he went to his peers or the captain, but he took care of it, just as he said he would.

You learn more on a cruise with a battle group than on independent ops where your ship is sailing alone. I flew to the carrier every two or three days for different reasons–transfer parts or supplies, pick up mail, deliver personnel for medical treatment–the helicopter was the easiest way to move people or cargo from ship to ship.

I got to land on every type of ship out there, not only our carrier but Marine LHA and LPH helicopter carriers. I landed on tankers and oilers. The tanker crews loved when the helicopters landed. There are safety crews aboard for flight operations who don't get the extra hazard pay unless there's a helicopter landing on board. We'd call and ask, "Do you need practice ops?" And they'd always say yes. So we'd land, they'd qualify for extra pay, and we always got a great lunch with the tanker crew.

The flight deck of a carrier is an airport squeezed into the area of five football fields. It's like driving in New York - you can kill yourself or others if you're not paying attention. If you get the call, "Cleared direct to carrier," you beat feat because that window is only open briefly, and if you're late, the carrier air boss will punish you by putting you in the purgatory of a holding pattern until he's ready.

For fixed wing aircraft, the carrier heads into the wind to increase the flow of air over their wings and give them extra lift. Usually they did the same for helicopters, but on one occasion, the air boss said they couldn't put her into the wind because they were on the way to some rendezvous and they didn't have time to deviate from that course. So instead of the standard approach, he said to come around the bow and land on the starboard side. This is irregular, and there's no procedure. So I said to myself, "Okay, Merryl, time to do that pilot shit."

So I flew around the bow of the carrier and came along the starboard side and I saw the spot I was supposed to land in. But the wind wasn't coming from the bow, as it ordinarily would–it was a crosswind. And my aircraft wasn't facing the bow, as it normally would, but aft. So I had to fly backwards to keep up with the carrier and then slide over to my spot and land in the very restricted space of *George Washington's* flight deck where the landing signal officer tells me to land. Which I did. You don't get to do stuff like that on independent ops.

## CONDITION ZULU

In October, we received orders to transit the Suez Canal and join the *Nimitz* battle group in the Gulf. The Suez Canal cuts through the desert. You look out and see these nomads walking across the sand, it smells awful, it's hot, desolate, sand blowing over the ship. Every seven days you have to wash the helicopter because the salt air and sand can really do a number on the engine and mechanicals.

Long deployments force you to be resourceful when it comes to entertainment. We did drills constantly. There are different stages, or conditions, of watertight integrity. Condition X-Ray means most hatchways are open. Condition Yankee is in force in port, some hatches are closed. Condition Zulu is the highest degree of watertight integrity where all hatches are closed. This would correspond with battle stations or an environment where the ship is a likely target. The aviation detachment's responsibility in Condition Zulu is to make sure hatches in our section of the ship are secured.

Stairways on Navy ships are called ladders, and for good reason. They are usually vertical or near vertical. Rock and I had just come up one ladder to the flight deck and our job was to close the hatch we had just passed through. But Lt. Cmdr. Blaisdell was coming up behind us. We both reached down and extended our hands to pull him up through the hatch. So I had one arm and Rock had the other and as we lifted him, Blaisdell's feet were no longer on the ladder. He was just dangling in mid-air.

I looked at Rock, he looked at me, and we smiled. As we pulled Blaisdell up with our left hands, we pummeled his legs with our right hands. He couldn't do anything about it since he was dangling. After a little of this torture, we pulled him up the rest of the way, laughing like hell. Blaisdell chased after us. Like the story about two people running from the bear, I didn't have to be faster than Blaisdell, I just had to be faster than Rock. Blaisdell caught him and got him down on the deck. And the flight deck has a no-skid surface, sort of like industrial sand paper, so when they were through, Rock had a few bruises and an impressive case of road rash. It cleared up by the time we returned home on April 3rd.

That deployment taught me never to let my guard down, to always be ready for the unexpected. And I learned that a female serving on a ship must be very careful about any kind of relationship with a man, married or single—even a casual friendship. Rumors can spread and get out of control quickly, so they must be addressed directly and immediately. Those lessons would prove useful later in my career.

## SECOND DEPLOYMENT

In the SH60B, the HAC is in the right seat, the H2P on the left. The H2P is usually also the airborne tactical officer, the ATO. As ATO, I was in charge of the tactical assets, launching the sonobuoys, deploying weapons, figuring out how to accomplish our mission. The control panel for those systems is on the left side of the cockpit, so that's where the ATO sits. The ATO determines how to approach a particular submarine. If we are working with a P-3, a land-based anti-sub aircraft, the ATO is the liaison between the two aircraft, deciding who will be responsible for what, which aircraft will deploy which weapons, and how to coordinate our efforts as a team.

The crewman in the back of the SH60B can be a great asset if you treat him correctly and keep him engaged in the mission. If he's pissed off at you he'll just sit back there like extra luggage and not lift a finger. If I'm a HAC and you think you're just coming along for the ride, that would be the last time you fly with me.

But if a pilot makes the effort to integrate the crewman into the mission, it pays huge dividends. Air crew are rescue swimmers, so on a search and rescue mission, they jump out of the aircraft into the water. They operate the rescue hoist from the back. They have an M60 automatic weapon they can fire from that position, they can drop flares, they're crucial to anything you do. There has to be mutual trust between the pilots and the crew. You have to talk quite a bit, especially if you're prosecuting a submarine or surface threat. You have to be able to communicate effectively within the aircraft.

Between deployments, I qualified as a HAC. It was a lot of studying and check flights, then an appearance before a board of peers who review your record. But I made the grade.

## TORPEDOES

There was an annual requirement to qualify for deploying torpedoes. This was done by dropping a live torpedo (without a warhead) from the helo and engaging a moving target. Andros Island in the Bahamas was the location for this exercise because it had deep water close to shore. While we were there for torpedo qualifications, we got a call from the Coast Guard to help look for a missing child. This was a real situation, not a training scenario. I was a HAC by then, but the pilot in the left seat was also very experienced. We had a senior crew man in back. It was a tense situation, but we had the skills and experience to handle it.

The second pilot, who was used to being a HAC, started arguing with the crewman about what type of search pattern we would run to find the missing kid. All communication is through mic and headphones, so everything is happening in my ear. And they're arguing back and forth while I'm flying the aircraft. "Go left, go right. Fly here, fly there." We were at 200 feet, yanking and banking, and all this chaos was going on in my ears. If we made a mistake, there wasn't enough altitude to fix it. It was a total goat rope.

Finally, I couldn't take it any more. Even though the other pilot outranked me, I had to be assertive. "STOP! One person talk to me. I'll put this aircraft where you want it. Just shut your hole."

I was tired and a little cranky. But they knew their behavior was unprofessional and unacceptable. It's nothing personal, it's business. When you work with the same pilots and crew for six months or more, depending on each other to accomplish the mission and keep everybody safe, you get to know people well. I like the feeling of teamwork with people you can depend on.

The one pilot who almost put us in the water was the only one I didn't get along with. He always acted like he was trying to prove something. He was arrogant. I was supposed to be learning from him, but I already knew more than he did. Still, we had to work together and fly together, so you adjust to people's strengths and weaknesses. I liked most everyone in my helo community. Even that dip shit.

## DETACHMENT 8

For the next deployment, I would be maintenance officer for Detachment 8 of our squadron. I was in charge of the fifteen enlisted personnel who kept the single SH60B aboard the USS *McInerney* in airworthy condition.

The maintenance guys were good and knew their jobs, and when I came aboard, they demonstrated cohesion and teamwork. The maintenance chief, highest ranking of the enlisted personnel, did not like me at first, and never did. I don't think he wanted to serve under a female officer. He wouldn't be the last person in my military career who felt that way, but as time went on, I learned how to deal with that attitude.

An opportunity to demonstrate my ability in my new role came immediately. The *USS McInerney*, FFG 8, was the oldest frigate in the fleet at that time. The Navy must have figured that the oldest frigate deserved the oldest helo, because the helicopter for Detachment 8 was not in flyable condition. It was a hangar queen, which is an aircraft that has awaited necessary repairs so long that it becomes a permanent fixture in the hangar. Soon it becomes a parts donor to other aircraft, and eventually it becomes an empty airframe, like cars you'd see in the Bronx, up on blocks with all the wheels, engine and electronics stripped out.

This SH60B hadn't reached that stage yet, but many of the parts had been stripped off, it was covered in bird poop, and its engines hadn't been started for quite a while. It looked like one of those before pictures of some classic muscle car uncovered in a barn in Indiana. It had potential, but that's about all.

We had five weeks to turn this barn find back into a flyable aircraft. I wondered if it was even possible, but I set my maintenance team to work, and a lot of them were new guys. They swarmed over that helo like a pit crew at the Indy 500. The aircraft needed almost everything, and I didn't ask where all the parts came from. They busted their asses. Finally they told me it was time to start those engines that had been idle for so long. I got in and wound her up. The engines started and ran sweet. It was a miracle.

There's a rotor brake that allows you to run the engines without engaging the rotor blades. I took off the brake and the rotor blades began to rotate and the helo vibrated like I was in the pilot seat of a washing machine. I shut it down because the blades hadn't been balanced yet. But that helicopter had been fully restored in a very short time by a dedicated team. It passed inspection and was ready for sea when we deployed. I was proud of those guys.

## DUAL GENDER CREWS

The Navy was still in the transition to dual gender crews, and *McInerney* was smaller than the cruiser, with a crew of 200, and much less space. I was one of two female officers on board - myself and a female H2P - and we shared quarters. But there was no female washroom. We shared the male officers' washroom, just like on *Ally McBeal*.

Guys would be in the shower and I'd go in to use the head and I'd have to say, "Hey, don't come out of the shower." Worse, guys would pee on the toilet seat. I knew they did it on purpose. I didn't want to clean up after them. I'd come into the wardroom after that. "What the fuck?" They'd laugh. And I'd say, "That's funny? How would it be if I peed in your Cheerios?"

The female H2P was my little protégé. I was hard on her because Gramps was hard on me. She had the potential to be a better pilot than I was, and I wanted her to make the most of that. I made her cry a couple of times. She probably hated me. But my job was to teach her things, to get her ready to be an aircraft commander, and not to let her settle for less.

We were together for a month of work-up cycles, then the four month cruise to South America. She left the SH60B community after her fleet tour and went to another aircraft, and did search and rescue. I'm sure she did well. She's a good pilot. My first instructor was hard on me, cursing me out a lot. I'm not like that on other people, but when I'm training someone, I am no nonsense, matter of fact, very short with my words. That can be a little scary for some. I'm from the Bronx. I can get that look that says, "I'm gonna kill you." The look is intimidating, but it isn't really dangerous. But my friend Liz says - it is when I stop yelling and get very quiet that it's about to go down.

## SOUTH AMERICA

Our second deployment was part of UNITAS, an annual exercise to improve military cooperation with Latin American states. We would be circumnavigating South America - Puerto Rico, through the lochs in Panama, then to Colombia, Ecuador, Peru, down through the Straits of Magellan, then back up and hit Brazil, then Venezuela and back home.

I don't think a lot of Americans understand what it really means to be poor. I didn't until we went on that second deployment. We were in either Peru or Chile, having lunch. I was with a couple of my maintenance guys and some other officers.

There was a "juicy" with us. A juicy is one of the prostitutes that followed UNITAS crews around. She probably made more during the four months of that exercise than she did all year. This girl was with one of our single guys. I knew who she was because I'd seen her in a previous port. I didn't care, I don't judge.

Whenever you're eating lunch in South America, you're always surrounded by a bunch of kids coming up and asking for money. They're a pain in the ass. I'm always like, "Get away from me. I got no money. Go away." I wasn't rude, but I didn't want to encourage them, either.

If they don't get any money, they just stand on the side, waiting for us to be done, watching us like hawks.

When we finished eating, this juicy had some leftover rice. She took her plate of rice and handed it to one of the kids. He scooped the rice up in his hands and then turned to his friends and let them all dip in, so they all got a little bit. Americans think we have people who are poor in the streets, asking for money. Most of the time those guys are scamming, making sixty grand a year. Some of them are drug addicts, some of them are legitimately poor. But there is a percentage who are not. They're making money and not paying taxes. It dawned on me that day after we finished our lunch that those little handfuls of rice were probably the only meal those kids were having that day. I felt like an ass, an ugly American. From then on, when kids asked for money, they got money. As long as it was just a few at a time, because if you give to one they come at you in a flock, like pigeons. Spare change to me is like the world to them. Maybe their parents won't beat them that night, if they have parents. Maybe they'll have a place to sleep.

It put poverty in a whole new perspective for me. When you see cardboard box shanty towns where people live in these terrible conditions, and they're still happy and still polite, you learn a lot. People need to get out and see that for themselves. And do it more routinely, than not.

## SAILOR LIFE

We stayed in certain ports for a day or two. Vendors knew we were coming, they put up their stuff to sell, that's fine. They make money on the tourists. But I made sure we had a Spanish speaker in our group when we went ashore. And I told that person to ask the same question every time—Where do the locals hang out? I always do that. I don't want to be on the beaten path. I want to be in that maze going into some unexplored alcove.

One of my enlisted maintenance guys was from Panama, machinist mate Rojas. He spoke Spanish. To the chagrin of the OIC, we used to go out on the town together. Officers and enlisted people aren't supposed to pal around. But none of the officers wanted to do what I wanted to do. I wanted to be a sailor. Rojas and I actually won a merengue contest in Chile.

. . .

The other officers, especially the other female officer, didn't want to go off the boat. I feel like they were uncomfortable in South America. I think it's because they were white and there were a whole bunch of Hispanic people making fun of them. Now you know how I feel when I go to frigging Europe.

So we were in Argentina and Rojas found out about a local spot. In Argentina, they speak Spanish, but they're racist AF. We're in South America, but in this crowd there were a lot of red-headed, blonde haired, blue eyed people. Argentina has many people of European descent because so many came over during the 1940s. There's a big German influence. I walked in with Rojas. His skin was lighter than mine, but still dark. It was just like a movie - these two dark skinned people come through the door in this white hangout and the music stopped. Really, it stopped. Everybody was looking at us. We were like, "*Que tal, ya'll.* What's up?"

It was fun to be in South America. I loved seeing the Andes. The further south we got, the shorter the people got. In the Straits of Magellan we actually stopped to trade spices and flour with the crew of a native fishing boat for some of their fresh catch. It was run by a couple of families. They were great people. I enjoyed Ecuador. Brazil is overrated. We were in Ipanema for a while. I don't like the people. They're a pain in the ass.

The beaten path is boring. I wanna go somewhere different where you have to rely on forming a connection with people. If everyone's been there and done that, I don't care. I want to see something that's not been seen before. I want to immerse myself in the culture. Not that I will become a local, but for that brief moment in time it helps me understand.

# 12

## FROM THE FLIGHT DECK

A COUPLE of incidents that may have had a major influence on my later career happened during that deployment. One was at the beginning of the cruise when we were off the coast of Colombia. The galley on *McInerney* had a dumbwaiter to deliver food between decks. One of the sailors working in food prep stuck his head into the dumbwaiter shaft and the dumbwaiter car fell and struck him in the head. It was a serious injury, and after our doctor got him stabilized, he recommended getting the injured man to a facility ashore where he could be treated by specialists.

Navy facilities were out of range, but fortunately there was a Navy Admiral on a visit to Colombia and he had a Navy jet that was ready to return to the United States. All we had to do was transport the stabilized patient from the ship to the Colombian airstrip and transfer him to the admiral's plane.

That sounded easy, until we learned that the admiral's plane was not at a big airport, but rather a small inland air strip in the jungles of Colombia. We had just left the port of Cartegena when the accident occurred, so we were close, but again this was before the age of GPS. We would have to navigate with map and compass.

The pilot in command (PIC) was Oscar, our OIC, in the left seat. I was in the right seat. We also had a crewman and a medical person to accompany the patient. We took off, flying low over the Colombian jungle, looking for this air strip. Every so often we'd pop up to get a better view, but it looked like endless jungle.

We finally located the strip. At the time, the Colombians didn't like SH60Bs because it was the same type of helicopter the Navy and Coast Guard used to interdict illegal drug shipments. Our two countries didn't have the closest relationship. Looking down at the airstrip, it didn't have an official look at all–just a paved strip in the jungle with a few aircraft, including the admiral's plane, and a bunch of guys standing around with automatic weapons. I didn't recognize the uniforms. Who were they? Who owned the air strip? What were we getting into? It was like something out of *The A Team*.

Oscar was a lieutenant commander, an experienced pilot. I was not a big fan.

"I'm going to do a run-on landing," he said. "I haven't done one in a while."

A run-on landing is when a helicopter doesn't land vertically, but instead lands more like a fixed wing aircraft, coming in at a shallow angle and rolling to a stop. An occasion for this might be if an engine is losing power, the aircraft is overloaded, or at high altitude where the air is thin. None of these conditions was present at the time, but Oscar wanted to try a run-on landing anyway. The SH60B had wheels instead of skids, so it was capable of performing this maneuver.

But it was not necessary as far as I could see. I don't know if Oscar wanted to show off for the admiral or for the Colombians at the air strip, or just wanted to practice the maneuver. But this was not a controlled environment. At least it wasn't controlled by our side. I was all about getting in, getting the patient off, and getting out. I didn't like being on the ground surrounded by armed people who weren't necessarily on our side.

I also have this instinct that whenever you're enjoying anything too much, you tend to overlook things. Oscar was definitely enjoying this. We were coming in with a seriously injured sailor and he was going to show everyone how it was done. He was in the zone. But I had a nagging sense that something was wrong. I kept going over the check list in my head. Everything looked okay, but something wasn't right.

Oscar lined up for the approach, we're coming in for the landing, he's got a clear spot to do his run-on landing and finally, a few seconds before we touch down, I see it, way over on the left side of the instrument panel, in front of Oscar, a little light that showed that the parking brake was on.

Very calmly, I said, "Take the parking brake off."

The SH60B has brakes for its wheels because when you land on the deck of a ship, that deck may not be level. Depending on the sea state, it could be angled in any direction. You don't want to execute a perfect landing in your helicopter and have it roll off the deck into the sea. So most of the time the parking brake is set. The wheels aren't supposed to roll. Because the parking brake is always on, the parking brake light is always on. It doesn't look out of place, so it's easy to miss.

But in a roll-on landing, where the aircraft will purposely have forward momentum on the ground, landing with the parking brake set means the wheels don't roll. If we had landed with the brake on, we would have blown the tires. And I would not know where to look for replacement SH60B tires in the Colombian jungle. We would have been stuck there, and our hosts would have been gun-toting Colombians who didn't like us.

"Oh, shit." Oscar quickly released the brake and he executed the landing as intended. We were on the field no more than fifteen minutes, transferring the patient to the admiral's plane, and then out of there. I felt a lot better when we were back in the air.

At debrief, Oscar said, "I'm glad you caught that." At least he acknowledged that he fucked up. The injured sailor got to a Navy hospital. He recovered, but he never came back to the ship.

## NO ROOM FOR ERROR

It's easy to become complacent in an aircraft. You can never let yourself assume everything is going to be okay. You train the same way all the time, do things over and over so that when something is out of the ordinary, you get this feeling that something is not right. Usually you figure it out. Some people figure it out too late.

The other incident also involved Oscar. As maintenance officer, I was responsible for keeping our restored SH60B in good shape. Certain systems require maintenance after so many hours in the air. Our helo was due for a major maintenance that required removing the rotor blades. Once the service is complete, the rotor blades have to be reinstalled and then balanced. To balance, they have to be tested and that can only happen on the flight deck. There is no room in the hangar to test the rotor blades.

The sea was pretty rough that day. It wasn't just the bow plunging into waves, but water was breaking over the flight deck aft. The nets were out surrounding the flight deck to keep anyone from washing overboard. The nets extended horizontally so as not to interfere with flight operations. The wind was also strong. It was not a good day to be on a weather deck.

This was the day that Oscar decided that the rotor blades should be tested.

The helo was secured to the deck by a Recovery Assist Secure and Traverse (RAST) system. It's a moving platform on the flight deck that can assist in a helicopter landing and also reposition the aircraft on the deck or maneuver it into the hangar. The SH60B was attached to this platform with a cable, so even in the rough seas, the helo was secured.

But that didn't help the maintenance guys who were climbing all over the aircraft to complete the servicing. The ship was tossing, water was washing over the flight deck, wind was howling, and these guys were soaked, trying to work in exposed conditions. It was like trying to change a tire on a Tilt-A-Whirl inside a car wash.

I was inside the helicopter with my operations officer and a crewman because we would have to start the engine and test the rotor blades when the maintenance guys were through. My ops officer, who was very experienced, was seasick and the crewman wasn't feeling great either.

Oscar was in the LSO enclosure which is mostly below the flight deck with an enclosed observation canopy at eye level to observe flight operations. From that vantage point, he could stay out of the weather and observe the entire flight deck. I don't know if he saw what happened next, but he should have seen it coming.

A wave washed over the flight deck and knocked one of the maintenance guys off his feet. It had enough force to wash him across the deck. It was Rojas, my Panamanian liberty buddy, and I watched the water sweep him over the side.

I jumped out of the helo in time to see him climbing back onto the flight deck. The nets had caught him and prevented him from being tossed into the sea, but that was enough for me. I turned to the crew. "We're done! Put this aircraft inside!"

I didn't ask Oscar for permission, and that must have rankled him, because he questioned my order over the radio. I didn't answer on the radio because radio communication can be picked up by anyone aboard. I didn't want the ship's company to know there was a disagreement among the aviation officers. I got out of the helicopter and made my way across the heaving deck to the sheltered LSO shack where a very rankled officer awaited.

"What do you think you're doing?"

"We're done," I told him "Didn't you just see what happened to Rojas?"

"You need to tell your maintenance guys to stop dicking the dog." That's a Navy term which means that one is unproductive or wasting time. Oscar was saying that my guys who were risking their lives to perform scheduled maintenance in the middle of a storm on a tossing deck on his orders were not making a real effort to get the job done. If they had been slacking off, I'd have told them. But they weren't. They were trying to do an extremely difficult job under hazardous conditions. Oscar had said the wrong thing to me.

"Fuck you! They're working their butts off!" This was not the standard response to a superior officer's comment on a maintenance detail. In fact, some would characterize it as inappropriate and ill-considered.

I was angry because Oscar was putting a routine maintenance job over the lives of my maintenance crew. If my people do something wrong, I'll clean up the problem and take care of it in private. But I always fight for my people, especially when we'd almost lost one. Oscar gave me a letter of reprimand. Our relationship was strained thereafter.

## NO ROOM FOR EMOTIONS

At the end of my second deployment, I was performing at the top of my game. I had become a HAC before I was a lieutenant. I served in all departments and acquitted myself well, as reflected on my fitness reports. I was qualifying lieutenant commanders in night carrier landings.

It's a competitive environment in which you have to do well. I was ambitious and confrontational and I was wound tight. If you said something to piss me off, I had no qualms telling you that you were an idiot. I didn't hesitate to get into a fuck you match with anybody. If the other person didn't like that, we'd step outside and settle it Bronx style.

A lieutenant commander in my squadron told me one time, "Merryl, your problem is that you wear your emotions on your sleeve."

"NO, I DON'T!" My reaction was instantaneous and visceral. He just sat there and looked at me. After a few seconds, I realized that I'd just proved his point.

I said quietly, "Oh, I see what you're saying. You are correct, Sir."

When we came off of deployment, I became assistant weapons and tactics officer. Oscar was the squadron's training officer, my boss's boss. I didn't tell anyone about the Rojas story, but I knew Oscar was setting me up to fail.

One day he called me into a room for "counselling." There were two other white male officers there. I can read a room - I knew I was being set up. I had been doing excellent work, but he had nothing but criticism for me. The examples he cited were ridiculous. "When you pass me in the hallway you don't say 'Hi,'" and stuff like that. But Oscar was in charge of my fitness reports, and the one he gave me was lackluster. It was not based on my performance, but my "attitude."

The squadron commander was a black officer. That doesn't mean he should have automatically taken my side, but he should have at least been supportive. I flew with him on a trip to the Navy test pilot school at Patuxent River because I wanted to be a Navy test pilot. I told him what was going on with Oscar, but he did nothing about it.

There was a political environment that was able to reach out and snatch away my opportunities and make it look like my fault. It wasn't overt, but it was clear from my performance report that I would not be recommended for promotion, and I could also forget about becoming a test pilot. I don't know why he was sabotaging my Navy career.

Was it because I was a female?

Because of the color of my skin?

Because of my attitude?

Because I was a better pilot?

Because of what happened in Colombia?

Whatever the reason, it was a career killer.

## NEW ORDERS

One of my instructors at helicopter school had been Delgetti, a black male officer, a mentor. We were good friends in the helo community because there weren't that many black officers. He was a professional. You knew by the way he carried himself that he was going places.

I called Delgetti. I was hurt and angry. Delgetti was working for the Navy Bureau of Personnel (BUPERS) in Millington, Tennessee. He was aware of the situation and knew my commander. He knew I had done well because all my fitness reports had been above average, but now suddenly they were flatlining.

I told Delgetti I wanted a different job. I needed something completely new, something intriguing. I needed the unknown. He asked if I could be more specific. I said I was curious about how things worked in the Air Force. A week later he called and said he might have something but couldn't tell me exactly what it was. It involved training, but that's all he could say. I said I'd take it.

I knew the orders were coming, but I had to arrange with my current squadron to be released early. I went to the squadron commander again. He told me I'd have to get the okay from Oscar. The opportunity to get out from under the officer who was determined to ruin my career would depend on his willingness to do me a favor. It seemed unlikely, but the only way out was through him.

I went to Oscar and said, "Sir, I have transfer orders coming down and I request permission to leave early."

He must have loved having me in this position. "What kind of orders?"

I didn't really know, other than that it was an instructor position. That's what I told him.

"T-38s or T-37s?" T-37s were jet trainers built by Cessna that had the styling of a soccer mom van. T-38s were the jet trainers the astronauts used. They looked like fighters. They were cool. "T-38s are great," he said. "T37s are awful, noisy, pieces of crap."

"I don't know, Sir," I said truthfully. But I knew he wasn't going to let me go to some place I would like. "I think T-37s." That seemed to delight him.

"Oh, sure, you can go."

I got my early release and it turned out to be neither of the aircraft Oscar mentioned. My orders were to Corpus Christi for instructor training in the T-34, then to Randolph AFB in San Antonio for a year instructing in T-6s, then to Moody AFB in Georgia. The last two were Air Force installations but I would still be in the Navy.

# 13

# MUSIC, MARTIAL ARTS, AND MISSIONS

*I am peaceful up until the point of impact.*

DELGETTI HAD INTERCEDED JUST as I hit the wall, and it wouldn't be the last time. I was still hurt and angry as I headed for Corpus Christi. This was a time in my life when music brought me back from the brink and got me centered. I brought the Casio keyboard and my bass guitar with me and I wrote songs and played them to give my emotions an outlet.

The thoughts in my head came out as lyrics in song after song. Many of them referenced drowning, cloudiness, suffocation. *The future in front of me holds so much uncertainty. Performance of the past fogs the path paved in front of me...Struggling, choking, gasping for air, dropping to my knees, the end coming near."* The chorus of that song was more upbeat and determined. *"To reach the pinnacle I know I can't stop. Keep pushing myself to make it to the top. I made it this far, just a little more to do. I refuse to fail, I refuse to lose.*

For the chorus of another song, I just wrote "anger" over and over again. Reading these songs twenty years later I was surprised about the feelings I had. I didn't realize what I was going through, but now I see I was a little fucked up. I was having issues and didn't tell anyone. As a pilot, you don't want to show any weakness, you don't ever admit to having problems. You just contain it and hope it doesn't boil over.

Music has the power to change hearts and minds, to motivate or depress. It can change that mood or accentuate the mood you're already in. This was my way of detoxing from four years in the Navy where I was in that competitive zone. I would do anything to stay on top. I was being a jerk and an asshole.

## LEARNING RESTRAINT

Sometimes I minimize my emotional response to situations because I know my response will be volatile. I'm a physical person. Martial arts teaches me to stay centered. It's a positive influence. My first reaction to conflict is to go to a physical place with some one. I have to dial that back. Then I relive it. If something happens, I play it over and over in my head. How could that scenario have been different, could I have said that better? You have to know when to take the sword out. It can't be your go-to every time. As much as you want it to be, it just can't. I worked a long time on attaining that restraint. There are times I just want to grab a bat and beat somebody over the head with it. But I've learned there are other ways.

Another positive influence was getting back to the T-34. It's a sturdy aircraft. You can do things in that airplane that you can't do in others. When I came back for instructor training, I could delve more into the advanced characteristics of the aircraft that were out of bounds when I was a student. Now I could take the T-34 up by myself and do loops, barrel rolls, Cuban 8s, Immelmans, split esses. I couldn't do aerobatics in a helicopter, but the T-34 was more than willing to indulge me. It was freedom.

I like cross control departure. You put the aircraft in an out of control flight situation. It tumbles on all axes, just falls out of the sky. You learn the basics of aerobatics, how to recover from a spin, what to do if you depart from controlled flight. It's disconcerting and it's fun. And it's reassuring to know how to fly out of a spin. That's what I was doing in Corpus Christi. I was flying out of a spin and regaining control of my life.

After completing instructor training at Corpus Christi, I transferred to Randolph AFB, right up the road in San Antonio. There I evaluated course structure for the T-6 trainer and went through pilot instructor training.

I also got back into martial arts. There was a school in Corpus Christi, Dragon Martial Arts, that taught wing chun, a form of kung fu from southern China. I'd do T-6 training for twelve hours, then study wing chun from six to nine, then turn in and start all over the next day. I was trying to get back to center, trying to find myself. Working out is a purifying process. If I'm uncomfortable or wrestling with some issue mentally, I can get into this transcendent zone, almost to the point of exhaustion. If there's music, even loud music, I won't even hear it. Every time I felt tired I would just push harder. You get so tired, every part of your being is thinking about that particular moment. There are no distractions. Sparring was even better. If you're in the ring, you can only concentrate on one thing - the opponent.

## SEPTEMBER 11TH, 2001

One morning I was sitting on the couch before going to work and there was a news interruption. I saw smoke billowing out of one of the towers of the World Trade Center. What the hell is going on? I was on the phone with Kjell when the second plane hit.

My mom worked at the post office in lower Manhattan, close to the WTC. I ended my call with Kjell and tried to get her on the phone, but I couldn't get through. It was not a good time. When I finally reached her later, she told me she had moved to a different branch uptown a couple of months before. She had been nowhere near the twin towers.

I had a friend, Eric Cranford, whom I knew from SH60B days. He was a senior lieutenant, a good guy. When my mouth would get me into tight spots, Eric usually helped get me out of them and smooth things over. When Kjell and I were dating, we would double with Eric and his girlfriend.

Eric had recently started a job at the Pentagon, briefing top officials. He was in the Navy section of the building where the third plane hit. He's buried at Arlington with a lot of other good guys.

## NO NEW NORMAL

The following month I transferred to Moody AFB in Georgia as a Navy T-6 instructor. The world had changed. I thought I was centered and back to normal. Then I had a student that really pissed me off.

He had been in the civilian world for a while and then decided he wanted to be a jet pilot. He was a little older than most of the students who were just out of college. He had some attitude. I exercised a lot of self control around this clown. I soloed him. He was at the end of the course and he found out that he didn't have enough points for jets. So he quit.

I was beside myself for a week. Did he know how many people work really hard to even qualify as a Navy pilot, how many people would trade anything to become a naval aviator? This clown comes in and says, "Oh, I can't be a fighter pilot? I quit." I was disgusted. He quit because he didn't get his first choice. I wanted him out of my sight. Then I wrote a song about him. It had a real 80s feel.

*"I see failure in your eyes. Your will is lost. Your strength is gone. You try to move on but can't. Thoughts of losing flood your mind. The smell of fear permeates your skin. I taste the end coming near."* Then the chorus: *"Quitter, you're a quitter, below average at best. Quitter, you're a quitter, make room for the rest."*

I realized that I wanted to be deployed. I didn't want to be instructing snot nosed millennials with attitudes. I wanted to be in a squadron, at sea, flying missions. I wanted to be in the fight.

• • •

Despite all the songs and aerobatics and martial arts, I was still easily irritated and restless. I realized what the last deployment with HSL48 had done to me. All the competitiveness and conflict put me on edge and made me brittle. I had just turned 30 and I was trying to get back to who I used to be. I didn't know that process would take several years.

My boss at Moody was Lt. Col. Mike Senna. Imagine a crusty old Marine officer in an Air Force uniform, and that's Mike Senna. He dipped, he smoked cigars, he cursed and he was crude. But he always took care of his people, of which I was one. We flew together at Moody. He was fun to work for and I valued his judgment.

"Merryl, you should join the Air Force," he told me. I was curious about how things worked in that branch and I had been working on Air Force bases for the last couple of years. He told me about an opportunity that might interest me. I would have to clear some hurdles, but on the other side was a chance to fly higher than I ever had before.

*Merryl, aged 14*

*Merryl and her Grandmother, Graduation Day*

*Kjell and Merryl in Date Mode*

*Wedding Day*

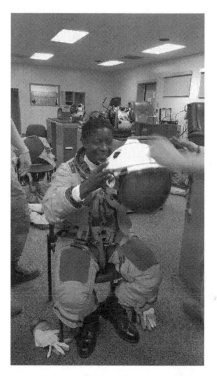

*Suiting Up*

*Merryl and Crew*

*Merryl with Flynn, Final Flight on the U2*

*Kjell, Merryl, and Mom, in 2013 Distinguished Alumni Award Ceremony.*

*Merryl, with her kids*

*Merryl, in her Next Mission as a Fitness Professional and
Motivational Speaker*

## Part Three

# SILVER WINGS

# DRAGON LADY

*You've got to fight the Dragon,*
*To dance with the Lady.*

KJELL SAYS that he suggested that I become a U2 pilot long before
Lt. Col. Senna urged me to trade uniforms. I don't remember it
that way, but maybe he's right. Whoever came up with the idea,
I decided to apply to the Air Force with the goal of becoming a
U2 pilot.

The U2 aircraft is an extremely unique and difficult plane to
learn to fly. It flies at an extremely high-altitude, at about 70,000
feet, with a very long range. As pilots, we have to wear the pressure suit for the duration of the flight. It's a single seat aircraft,
which is unique in itself. And its one of the more challenging
aircrafts to land, because of the bicycle landing gear configura-
tion. In order to land, you've basically got to stall at two feet - no
drift, no crab, and visibility is very limited. Flying the U2 aircraft
is not intuitive to most pilots. It's physically uncomfortable and
physiologically exhausting. It's not for everyone. It's definitely
not for the faint of heart.

The U2 aircraft is famous for being difficult, which is why it
earned the nickname - Dragon Lady.

Amongst the community of U2 pilots, of which there are only about 1,100 of us, there have been ten women who have been qualified to fly.

I'm the first and only black woman.

Of black pilots, there may only be about ten.

I am a rare unicorn on the Dragon Lady.

That's why I've also earned the nickname - Dragon Lady.

## PERSONAL ACCOUNTABILITY

*Growth is impossible without personal accountability.*

Anyone who knows how the military works will not be surprised at the ensuing paperwork snafu. I was told that before I could join the Air Force, I would have to leave the Navy. That made sense. An officer accomplishes that by formally resigning her commission, in writing. I sent a letter to the Navy resigning my commission and a letter to the Air Force requesting a commission. I also sent a letter to the commander of what I hoped would be my new station, Beale AFB, in California. It all seemed very straightforward.

The Navy granted my resignation. That was easy. Then the Air Force responded and said what I was requesting was an interservice transfer, but since I had resigned from the Navy, I was no longer eligible. Interservice transfers are only available to active service members, and with my resignation, I was now transitioning into a civilian.

I quickly sent another letter to the Navy asking to rescind my resignation so that I could stay in the Navy long enough to join the Air Force. While I was waiting for that answer, I got a message from Beale. They were inviting me to interview to be a U2 pilot.

## U2 PILOT

The U2 is a high altitude reconnaissance jet aircraft that was designed in the 1950s and used initially by the CIA to keep a high eye on Russian ICBM sites. It looks like a big black glider.

Every military aviation specialty has unique requirements and the U2 community is no exception. The U2 patch includes the Latin phrase *"solum volamus,"* which means "Alone when we fly." The U2 carries no weapons, only cameras and sensors, so the other phrase that applies would be, "unarmed and unafraid." The idea was to design an aircraft that flies too high to be shot down. Unfortunately, that concept was disproved with the first loss of a U2 to a Soviet surface-to-air missile over Sverdlovsk in 1960.

U2 pilots spend long hours high over enemy territory in an aircraft that was designed before most of its pilots were born. In flight the pilot wears a pressure suit, like a space suit, to supply her with oxygen and to protect her in case the pressurized cabin is compromised. This is a very restrictive and claustrophobic garment, and not everybody is comfortable in it. The U2 is the only aircraft in the Air Force inventory that requires a pilot to wear a pressure suit.

Training to fly the U2 takes about a year, so the Air Force wants to make sure that anyone they spend that much time and effort on is going to be a good fit with the quirky people of the U2 community. Therefore, there is a two-week "interview" that aims to eliminate anyone who might not be solum volamus-minded.

During the first week, I interviewed with the commanders of the 1st RS, the training squadron, and the 99th RS, the operational reconnaissance squadron which can be deployed anywhere in the world. I visited the operations group commander to get a feel for the program and so they could get a feel for me.

I was measured for a pressure suit and liner. Then I went through a claustrophobia check. In this exercise, they sealed me inside the pressure suit and helmet, sat me in a chair, and left me alone for an hour. It was very much like being in a sensory deprivation chamber. All I could hear was the hiss of the oxygen flow and my own breathing and heartbeat. The average person is usually unprepared to spend that much time alone with herself. But I was like, "Hey, Self. Whatcha doing?" It was actually very relaxing. After a little while, I fell asleep. I had no issues chilling in the suit.

There were a lot of other tests, interviews, and evaluations the first week. The second week was my introduction to the aircraft. I went on three flights with two different instructors; Doug Dillard and Duane Dively, also known as "Muff." They were trying to determine if I could be taught to fly the aircraft, how quickly I could learn, and if I had the skills, personality and commitment to be a U2 pilot.

## POWER AND PITCH

On my first two flights, Doug was the instructor in the aircraft with me and Muff was my mobile (a position I will explain below). Those first two flights, my performance was about average. Wing control was giving me all kinds of problems. The U2 has unusually long wings, like a glider, and a pilot has to keep them level on landing because the wingtips will scrape if she doesn't.

I had one more interview flight, and this time Muff was in the aircraft and Doug was the mobile. I knew I had to fly better than I did on the first two flights to be admitted to U2 training. Muff knew I was frustrated and that this was my last chance.

• • •

Every aircraft has guidelines for the pilot which should yield optimum performance. For example, a guideline might tell a pilot the ideal speed for takeoff or the minimum altitude for a certain maneuver. The two most important variables are power and pitch. Power refers to engine power output. Pitch describes the position of the aircraft relative to an imaginary horizontal axis that is perpendicular to the fuselage. The aircraft rotates on this axis so that if the nose goes up, the tail goes down, and vice versa.

The U2 had such guidelines, and in my interview flights I was struggling to keep the aircraft within those guidelines. This is what pilots call "flying the numbers." I was on a normal approach pattern, trying to force the aircraft to stay within the guidelines of power and pitch, not to mention all the other variables.

I heard Muff's calm voice in the headphones. "How does this look?"

To me, it seemed we were lower than we should be, but I was within the guidelines. "Looks a little low."

Then he said something profound. "Then fix it."

That's all he needed to say. When I was an instructor on the T-6 I would tell my students that you can learn all the power and pitch values in the world, but they're just guidelines. The ultimate decision is up to the pilot. What Muff was telling me was to forget the guidelines and just do my pilot thing and fly. My flight got much better after that.

## THE U2 COMMUNITY

Muff became a friend. He had an artistic side. We both liked music. He was a Pink Floyd fan, he built amplifiers and, like me, he played bass. He was former Marine enlisted, then switched over to the Air Force. He was well thought of in the U2 community. He had a very dry sense of humor. And he saved my final interview flight, because at the conclusion of the two-week process, I got an invitation to join the U2 community.

The Navy had reinstated my commission, but the last thing I'd heard from the Air Force was "no thanks." So when I got the invitation from Beale to join the U2 squadron, I sent that to the Air Force Personnel Center along with my rescinded Navy resignation paperwork, and I was finally commissioned as a brand new Air Force major select. (Major select meant that I was in line to be promoted to major.)

I reported to Beale AFB in northern California for training. Flying the U2, you have a "mobile," another U2 pilot who is like a wing man on the ground. He sets up the cockpit for you and goes over the preflight check lists. For high altitude flights, he does the walk around because you're already in the suit and you don't want to walk around the airplane in a pressure suit– you'd look like a dork. For low altitude flights for which the pressure suit is not necessary, the pilot does the walk around herself.

All pilots serve as mobiles to other pilots, so teamwork and trust are vital. The mobile's job before the mission is to prepare the aircraft to the pilot's specifications. Some pilots took advantage of this. One guy's list of things he wanted in the cockpit was a foot long. "I want the pedals 3/4 front to back. I want four water bottles on the left and three Gatorades on the right. I want the tube food set up in this order..."

Since we fly in pressure suits, we can't just flip up the helmet visor and munch on a sandwich. The physiological support detachment (PSD) gives us food in toothpaste tube-like containers with a straw that can be inserted through a port in the helmet. When you squeeze the container the contents, reduced to the consistency of baby food, go through the straw into your mouth. We drink the same way. But this pilot wanted key lime pie first, then chicken a-la-king, then the peach cobbler, in that specific order. It was too much. I avoided being his mobile whenever possible.

My list for cockpit set-up was brief. I wanted the pedals at half way and the seat at half way, because I'm short. That was it.

On the morning of the mission, the pilot and mobile meet two hours and fifteen minutes prior to a flight. The charts for the route have been prepared the day before and include checkpoints, speed, altitude and fuel requirements to monitor the progress of the flight. They will tell you if you reach this checkpoint, you should be going at this speed and altitude, have this much fuel left, and so on.

The crew chief is responsible for the aircraft and supervises the ground crew who turn it around. There's a binder that records anything that has happened to the aircraft, all the maintenance that's been done, anything that has put the aircraft out of commission and the corrective action taken. The mobile will go over that book with the crew chief. When the pilot is integrated into the aircraft, the crew chief will hand her the book and she will sign it to officially accept the aircraft. The crew chief salutes the pilot. I always shake hands with the maintenance guys who put the aircraft together. Sometimes I hug them.

Ninety minutes prior to the flight, the pilot goes to the PSD, strips down to her underwear, and then two people integrate her into the liner and the pressure suit and make sure everything is working. The pilot goes on 100% oxygen an hour before take off to prevent decompression sickness (DCS). Forty minutes prior to takeoff, PSD people drive the pilot out to the flight line and integrate her into the aircraft, again confirming that the pressure suit is operating normally. They make sure all the pilot's physiological needs are taken care of.

Twenty minutes prior to takeoff the pilot starts the engine. Ten minutes prior, the pilot taxis out to the runway. At Beale, it only takes about two minutes. The takeoff time must be exact so that the pilot hits all the checkpoints at the right time.

. . .

After the mission, the pilot calls the mobile an hour before her return to base. The mobile gets into a high performance car and waits near the runway threshold. As the U2 crosses the runway threshold, the pilot will rely on the mobile to tell her how far above the runway she is so that she can make a smooth landing. The U2 windscreen is so small, and the helmet limits the pilot's visibility to such an extent that it's hard to pick up visual cues outside. If you stall at four feet instead of two feet, you can break the aircraft. In addition, the U2 has a bicycle landing gear arrangement—large wheels forward in the fuselage, smaller wheels toward the back, and no other gear. If the pilot doesn't land with wings level, a wingtip could dip and be damaged by contact with the runway.

The mobile will watch the approach of the U2 and then floor the accelerator in order to match the U2's landing speed of approximately 100 miles per hour. The mobile in the car follows the aircraft closely as it descends and reports the distance from the runway to the tires, in feet, as it settles onto the pavement.

"Six...four..two...one..." Even though the U2 has landed, the pilot is still flying and the mobile is still keeping her apprised of her situation. "Raise right" means your right wing is dropping, for example. I had a tough time with wing control. I kept teeter-tottering so much that I wore out the tail wheel and it had to be replaced. It happened to me twice. Tail wheels and I just did not get along.

It's possible to land without a mobile, especially with experience, but it's much safer with a mobile. In the U2, everyone is pretty experienced. I trusted their expertise. It wasn't like the helicopter days when I had an aircraft commander who was mediocre. Most of these U2 pilots have 500 hours of instructor time, 1500 hours of total time. But the no flap landing we do in the U2 is a dangerous procedure. It's a shallow approach and the stall margin is plus or minus two knots. If you hit a thermal on approach at 100 feet, you'll be in trouble. It's a handful of aircraft. And she'll kill you very quickly if you become complacent. Maybe that's why the aircraft earned the nickname, "Dragon Lady."

I was never one to be complacent, and I had two experienced instructors who showed me a few other things that would keep me alive in the U2. They were John Huggins and Mike Means - Huggy and Means. The U2 is not built for aerobatics or high speed, but it has some amazing capabilities. Huggy and Means showed me how to get the most out of the Dragon Lady.

# LIFE, LOSS, AND LOVE

BY THE TIME I started my U2 training, Kjell and I had been long-distance dating for nine years. He was in the Navy reserves, an engineering officer. When I got picked up for the U2 program in California, Kjell entered a PhD program at UC Davis, about 45 minutes away. So we were finally in the same location and I was in training, so I wouldn't be deployed.

Toward the end of my training, Kjell wanted to celebrate by taking me to our favorite steakhouse. Steak was fine with me, but for some reason that night I was more in the mood for seafood. He hates seafood. But he couldn't talk me into the steakhouse, so we went to The Cannery for dinner.

He was in a romantic mood, but I was chowing down on Dungeness crab, smelling like fish, not paying much attention to him. He asked if I would like to order dessert. "Naw, I don't need dessert." This seemed to disappoint him. Then he asked if I'd like to sit next to him instead of across from him. "Naw, I'm fine over here." Everything he suggested, I had a contrary view. I could see he was getting frustrated.

"What's on your mind?"

"Basically, do you want to get married?"

"No way!" I didn't mean, "No way, I don't want to get married." I meant, "No way," like I thought he was messing with me. Then he pulled out the ring.

I said yes, and then added, "I gotta go to the bathroom." I went and called my friend Robin to tell her the news.

Don't tell my mom - she thinks I called her first.

The other big news was that in six weeks I was headed to Osan Air Base in Korea, on my first deployment as a U2 pilot.

*To do bigger things you need a small circle of friends.*

## LOSING A MENTOR

On my thirteen hour flight to Korea, I started thinking about Muff, my U2 interview instructor, who was deployed to the Middle East. I wondered what he was up to out in the desert. I got the very strong feeling that I should call him. When I got to Osan, they told me, "Muffy's dead. He crashed." He had gone down in his U2 while I was on my way to Korea. He was probably giving me a spiritual parting shot.

When Muff died the overall tone of the deployment changed dramatically. He had 2000 hours when he died in that aircraft. He's the reason I got hired into the program and he taught me a lot of things. At the time they didn't know the cause of the crash. Later we found out it was pilot error. He misdiagnosed a problem with his aircraft. He had lost power and hydraulics, so he thought he had engine failure. He was trying to trouble shoot, but he didn't have the altitude. He was at 2000 feet, at night. If he'd known he still had a working engine, he could have pushed up the power and he would have been okay.

It may have been that his experience worked against him. Since I was new to the aircraft, if I'd been in that same situation, I might have ejected. Two thousand feet, no power–I'm out of there. But Muff had 2000 hours in the U2. He tried to figure it out. That's what pilots do. At 15,000 feet, he might have had time to solve the problem. But at 2000 feet, the deck was stacked against him.

My first four missions in Korea, I came back every time because of malfunctions. I was 0 for 4. Physiologically it started to weigh on me - I couldn't seem to fly without something going wrong. Add to that the emotion of losing a friend. A guy like that, with all those hours in the U2, gets killed. What did that say about somebody like me who had 120 hours? It was a cloud hanging over everybody. It was tough. I was stressed out.

## CREATE NOT DESTROY

From my first deployment in the U2, everything I was going through weighed heavy on my mind. Compounded on my mind was that my friend Muff had just passed, all the malfunctions, and the physiological stressors were getting to me. I was going through a dark time. My outlet, when I am going through stressful times, is music. Instead of letting the dark place turn into something destructive, I channelled it into my creative expression. I tell my kids this to this day - learn to create not destroy. That changes the way you see things.

A couple of weeks into my deployment, I was up late. I started writing a song. It took about twenty minutes. *"It's 2 a. m. Can't sleep at night. Contemplating my whole life. Pressure's weight holds me down, future goals so distant now. Things are out of my control, I'm doing all I can. It seems to never be enough. Sometimes I want to give up. The shroud of darkness covers my face, the water rises, I can't breathe. For every step I take I get pulled back and never get to my feet...As daylight comes I fear today will be the day I'm pushed to the edge."*

I sent a copy to my mom. She called me, "Do you need to talk to someone? Are you okay?"

"They're just thoughts." Some of it was about me, some about what I saw others going through. "Mom, I'm just writing feelings down. I'm okay."

Maybe I should have been a poet instead of a pilot.

Or, a poet and a pilot.

## KOREA

Korea was my favorite deployment. Older Koreans really loved us for helping during the Korean War. I think they put up with our shenanigans because of that. They were very polite and grateful. I enjoyed talking with them. The younger generation doesn't like us as much. I saw things from the Koreans' perspective. It was enlightening.

I did the DMZ tour and got to see the infiltration tunnels started by the North Koreans as invasion routes. One of the reasons the old people liked Americans is that they remember what North Korea was like. Now North Korea is the world's most isolated country.

I just enjoyed Korea. It's the only southeast Asia country I've been to. I've done the Mediterranean, Middle East, South America. I don't really want to go to Japan. I would love to go to China but maybe that wouldn't be a good destination for a former U2 pilot. I'd rather go to Singapore. I'd like to see Africa. I've never been there. And Australia, I need to go to that continent.

I would love to check out the Great Wall. It's one of the few manmade structures you can see from space. I never saw it from the air. When you fly over South Korea the weather is terrible. There's weather from 30,000 to 45,000 feet. It's a big layer. I was there May through July and it was just hot, humid and crappy weather. I would like to check it out again and get off the beaten path. Maybe eat a couple of scorpions. No, just kidding, I'm not going to eat any scorpions.

Mongolia would be great to see. I wanna see some blonde haired Asian people. I've never seen one. It's between Russia and China, so there must be blonde haired Asian people there. If I went to Mongolia, people would freak out if they saw me. They would just touch my skin all day. When I did the DMZ tour all the Chinese people were staring at me. I was like, "Stop staring at me. You got partial internet, you can look at black people all day, stop staring at me."

Even when I was in Osan, I'd get the stares. On my days off I would go to the Bulgogi House, better known as the Mud Hut. After a mission, you don't fly the next day, you get to recuperate. I'd go to the Mud Hut and speak broken Korean and English with the owner and we'd just talk (or not talk), eat, drink, and just chill. I may not have understood him fully, but I could feel his emotion and passion.

When I hung out with other locals I found out that the military was not always a welcome presence. I was embarrassed because every night all these service members would get drunk and belligerent and out of control and the locals would call us "sul dwaeji." I asked a Korean lady what that meant and she told me, "Liquor pigs." I didn't want to be like that. I would drink, but I wasn't getting hammered.

There was an intelligence officer there who belonged to the LDS church. He'd gone on his mission to Korea, met his wife there, and spoke the language fluently. Mormons aren't supposed to drink. So we'd go to the bar and I'd sit at a table inside by the window with my alcoholic beverage and he'd sit at a table outside the same window with his soft drink and we'd just chill. I respected his habits and he respected mine.

We'd go running together and he taught me Korean. I learned a lot in two months. One of the things I learned was that wedding dresses are a lot cheaper in Korea. My LDS buddy came with me to order my wedding dress because he could describe exactly what I wanted to the Korean dress makers.

## 16

# PLANNING A WEDDING

*If you know yourself well, don't let other people's opinion change how you feel about you.*

WHEN I CAME BACK from Korea, Kjell and I locked down a venue and date. The wedding would be a civilian event, not military. The reception would be at the Arden Hills Country Club. There was a pleasant wedding planner there to work out all the arrangements. She had lots of questions I wasn't prepared for.

"What kind of bouquet would you like?"

I'd never been married before. How should I know? "Something with...flowers."

"What are your colors?"

I thought seeing me together with my fiancé, she would be able to tell we were black and white, but she meant the color scheme for the wedding. Again, I had no idea. But there was a wedding party there the day we were meeting, so I pointed at the bride's bouquet and said, "How about that one?"

We weren't really interested in an expensive, lavish wedding. Kjell wanted a good photographer, but we didn't want to go into any debt and we agreed that we'd spend the money on the honeymoon. For the wedding, I just wanted an open bar where I could be double-fisting beers and have a good time with family and friends.

## DEPLOYMENT BEFORE WEDDING

We nailed down all the arrangements, made reservations for a honeymoon in Maui, and were looking forward to our wedding - right after my second deployment, this time to the Middle East. I would be stationed at Al Dhafra, the same base from which Muff flew his last mission.

By this time, it was becoming evident that I was not on the fast track to astronaut. Even though I wore a pressure suit when I flew, it seemed unlikely that I would be going to space. But one night, space came to me.

I took off for my high flight at 11:00 p. m. There was no moon and the sky was clear, at least at 70,000 feet. By 2:00 a. m. I was flying along, enjoying the ride in my Lockheed U2. Then I saw a shooting star. ("Shooting Star" was also the name of Lockheed's first jet fighter, the P-80.) It appeared brighter and larger than the meteors I'd seen from the ground. It was not blinding, but it was beautiful. From my view, it seemed to be at a lower altitude than my aircraft. It was like a little message from outer space–"Hey, Merryl, what's up?"

As I reflected on the fleeting beauty of the fiery streak across the atmosphere, I had another thought. "That would have sucked if it had hit my aircraft."

## STATIONED IN THE MIDDLE EAST

My first mission to Afghanistan was to support troops who were engaged with the Taliban. I provided images that resulted in several enemy killed in action. When I returned to base, the OIC was all excited. He congratulated me and wanted to take me to the colonel so I could tell him all about it. But it was an eleven hour mission, not counting the prep time. I was tired. I just wanted to sleep. To me, I was fighting for my cause and they were fighting for their cause. I don't revel in killing people. I do it without hesitation, because that's my job, but I don't celebrate it.

Before I left for Al Dhafra the second time, I met another U2 pilot, Heather Fox. She is from New York, just like me. But upstate, which is a world away from the Bronx. She is smart, funny and capable, and we've been friends ever since we met.

During my first long cruise deployment with the Navy, we had gone ashore at various ports, haggled with vendors, gone drinking and dancing at the local spots, even tried sand boarding in the desert. We had been in Dubai before it was cool. It was an earthier experience - we could hear, taste, smell and touch the unfamiliar.

For my Air Force deployment, we were in the United Arab Emirates. It was more westernized. This particular year, Ramadan and Christmas both fell in December, so at the big Marks & Spencer mall there was a giant Christmas tree. A Christmas tree in an Arab state. We usually stayed on base and didn't interact with the locals much. If we wanted to go into town, we had to get permission and we kept a low profile.

The U2 is an old design constantly being updated with new technology. On the other hand, old technology is also useful. Some of our missions involve providing images of the territory negotiated in the Camp David Accords. For that we use an optical bar camera that provides high resolution images of the ground, even though we fly twice as high as the average airliner. The optical bar camera uses photographic film because digital images are too easily manipulated. The U2 has capabilities no other aircraft can match.

We also use digital cameras for other missions. We transmit these images to a distributive ground station (DGS) for analysis and distribution to troops in contact or other forces in the area. Some pilots will communicate directly with troops on the ground and some will fly a whole mission without talking at all. I usually let circumstances dictate what communications I initiate. Mostly I try not to think about peeing in my suit.

On one mission over Iraq, I had twenty minutes left on station when I got a call that an American soldier had been taken hostage. The OIC wanted to know how quickly I could get to a certain point and set up a search pattern over a city. Every minute after a soldier goes missing is critical because the longer it takes to locate him, the lower the chances of retrieving him. I was at the end of my mission with no chance of refuelling. I had to figure out how much fuel I had and how long I could extend my mission and still get back home. I got to the city and started the search, extending by a half an hour, but that was it. I headed back and other assets took over the search.

On the way back, I was looking down at nothing but desert, and none of it friendly territory. It looked desolate and lonely. I thought about SERE school. Well, if I exhausted my fuel supply out there, at least I wouldn't get frostbite.

I returned to base and the soldier had still not been found. We flew searches for the next 48 hours. Ultimately, we found the soldier's remains. He had been killed by insurgents. The squadron was pretty down for a while after that.

## IF MERRYL EVER ASKS IF YOU'RE NAKED

Stationed in Al Dhafra, it was the only time I had a roommate on an Air Force deployment. Fortunately, I shared quarters with Heather Fox. She came in one time and I was sitting at the computer desk. I spun around and looked at her, showing no emotion at all.

"Is everything okay?" When my expression seemed frozen, she became a little concerned. Then I cracked a slight smile. She studied me for a minute and then realized no one was home. "Are you on ambien?" My smile got bigger and more devious. "Go to bed!"

At least that's the way Heather remembers it. I have to take her word for it, because I don't remember anything.

One that we both remember is the time a journalist interviewed her for Women's History Month. Heather has had a stellar career, working in policy and getting all kinds of awards and recognition. She's now the wing commander of Beale and is on her way to being a general. But this was before she was used to media attention and she was squirming a little bit. She kept trying to shift attention to me. "Why don't you ask Merryl? She's a U2 pilot, too."

And every time the interviewer would turn to me, I'd just sit there and do my Jedi mind tricks. "No, this is not the female pilot you are looking for." And attention would shift back to Heather. She was so mad.

Now she knows how to put the spotlight on me in any situation. She just tells the interviewer, "If Merryl ever asks if you're naked, the answer is 'Yes!'" And then I do get a lot of attention because I have to explain that.


Believe it or not, it can get cold at night in Al Dhafra. Ambien may have been involved on this occasion. My memory is hazy on that. I know that Heather was already in bed, bundled up in blankets. I was a little chilled. So I innocently asked, "Heather, are you naked?"

"Naked? No, I'm not naked."

And so I jumped into her bed and nuzzled up against her to warm up. This was not what she was expecting. But if she'd told me she was naked, I never would have done that. That's why Heather says, "If Merryl ever asks if you're naked, the answer is 'Yes!'"

## SAFETY FIRST

During my deployment with Heather, we got a new commander at the detachment. He decided to make safety a priority and emphasized this with a massive poster campaign. He printed up all kinds of motivational posters about safety and readiness and put them up all over the building.

About this same time there was a Jonah Hill movie called *Superbad* that had a teenaged character who was obsessed with drawing penises. Well this was just unfortunate timing, because somebody at our base who had obviously been deeply affected by the film started drawing penises on all the commander's safety posters. No one ever could figure out who the artist was.

The commander called us all together for a mandatory meeting in which he demanded to know who was defacing his safety posters. He showed an example, possibly more than one.

I was trying to keep a straight face, and turned away in case I failed. But when I turned, I happened to catch the eye of one of the female maintenance people and we both just burst out laughing.

The commander gave me the most evil look, like he wanted to choke the life out of me. But I couldn't help myself. It was hilarious, funnier than the movie. Most of the women deployed at the time felt the same way.

Right after that, on one of Heather's flights, I was her mobile. One of my jobs was to check her boards, or charts, before the mission. When I handed her the charts prior to her flight, I told her, "By the way, I drew a whole bunch of penises on your boards. When you check in to say you're safe in your location, you have to tell me how many there are, and I'll tell you if you got them all."

So Heather flew her mission and reported in when she was back over friendly territory. I was there to receive it, along with all the other people at the ground station. She completed her official report and then added at the end, "The number is 13."

I responded, "That is correct."

All the other people at the station were asking, "What is that? What was that figure? What's she talking about?"

I might have ignored their queries or given some non-answer. Or, I might have given them the impression that it was classified far above their level. In any event, I didn't tell them that it was just our private version of *Highlights for Children*. Find the hidden objects on the chart.

## 17

# SHATTER THE MOLD

AT THE END of my second desert deployment in 2006 I came home for my wedding to Kjell. It was the simple celebration we wanted with friends, family and free-flowing drinks. We followed that with a honeymoon which was, like all visits home between deployments, way too short.

On my next deployment, our U2 detachment was hosted by the Royal Air Force at Akrotiri, the British base on the island of Cyprus in the Mediterranean. Like most Greek islands, the view is spectacular. Cyprus is divided into two sides - Greek and Turkish. Akrotiri is on the Greek side. The Brits could not have treated us better - they were respectful and gracious. I befriended a Royal Navy officer there who knew all the best watering holes.

One type of mission we'd fly in Afghanistan would be to scout overland convoy routes. If a convoy was planning to take a certain road, we'd photograph that area on successive days to see if anything had changed—new structures, topographical disturbances, obstacles. If we found any of these that might indicate preparations for an attack, we'd suggest taking an alternate route.

. . .

When I was on *Normandy* with a crew that was almost all men, there was also a lot of porn. The maintenance guys built a loft in the hangar that was their off duty man cave. They had magazines and a TV up there. A bunch of men getting together to watch porn made me scratch my head, but if that's how they relaxed, okay. They liked to show me their *Playboy* centerfolds to try to get a reaction out of me, but it didn't upset me. It did start to get old after a couple of months, however.

I told my mom about the situation. She sent me a *Playgirl* magazine. So naturally I showed all the guys, just as they showed me their magazines. They were disgusted, but they stopped sharing their stuff with me. The *Playgirl* from home became a tradition on deployment. We had to suspend while I was in the UAE because that sort of thing is not acceptable there. However, when I got to Cyprus, Mom was back in the beefcake by mail business.

I took the latest issue on one mission from Cyprus. It had a great article about fitness expert Jack LaLanne. He was a very bright guy, really studied the human body and came up with all these different training methods. He invented the Smith machine, a weight lifting device where the weight is on a vertical track. It lets the user concentrate on lifting without worrying about the weight falling forward or back. So there I was, 70,000 feet over the eastern Mediterranean, kicking back and reading about Jack LaLanne. The idea of being a fitness trainer appealed to me. It was a sign of things to come.

## MY MOTHER'S MISSION

Coming back from the Middle East, I was on a layover in Michigan. I called my mom and she told me she was going to have brain surgery to remove a tumor. I knew nothing about this. So I got back to California, stayed for a day, then turned around and got back to New York just in time to see my mom getting wheeled into surgery.

. . .

When I got back to Beale, my group operations commander called me into his office. "Merryl, I've got something for you. I want you to be director of operations for the 9$^{th}$ Physiological Support Squadron." I looked at him and my eyes got wide.

"Sir, please don't do that to me." It was a step up, but I knew that the officer previously in that position had been fired for sexual misconduct. He was a married officer involved with an enlisted female under his command. The squadron was a hot mess.

"No, you'll be great, you'll get things done, it's a good thing."

"Sir, I don't want to."

"Merryl, you'll be okay."

I completely lost all my military bearing. "Come on, man. Please don't do this to me."

"Merryl, you're doing it."

I think he wanted me for the job because there were a lot of women in the squadron and he thought a female leadership presence would help clean things up. He was right, and I still didn't want to do it. It was a mine field. But it turned out to be one of the best jobs I ever had.

## DRAMA IN THE SQUADRON

The average age in the squadron was 26, so there were lots of young people, which means lots of drama and intersecting relationships. Some of the people had been with each other ten or fifteen years. It was not uncommon for a couple to be dating for years, and then break up, and then one person would be dating another person from the squadron and have kids by that other person, or be married to one person in the squadron and be dating another person. It was like *Peyton Place* or *90210*.

We had to pull one guy back from deployment because he was sleeping with another guy's wife while her husband was deployed. I had to separate the two men in the squadron because the physical violence that almost ensued the first time they met each other would have been pretty bad. We gave him an Article 15 (non judicial punishment, short of a court martial) and fined him. I'm not a big fan of taking money from young enlisted people because they're already working at the limit. But the situation he created was so egregious we had to pull him back and send out a replacement. It cost money to do all that.

It was common knowledge that the medical group commander was being deployed to Iraq for five or six months. My squadron commander was going to take the open spot, thus leaving the commander position in my squadron open. There were two majors eligible for that position - myself and another female officer. The other major felt that she was more qualified to be commander since her background was in physiological support and I was a pilot. But in the Air Force, pilots are rated qualified for any leadership position. When it became evident that one of us would be chosen, her words to me were, "If you get selected as the acting commander, I will have a serious problem with you."

I told her the decision was not up to me and whichever way it went, we'd both have to be professional and support each other. When the promotion went to me, she demonstrated that she had no intention of conducting herself in a professional manner.

Our first meeting after the promotion was supposed to be about preparing for an upcoming inspection. Instead, she turned it into a diatribe about how she'd been overlooked and under-appreciated. The worst was to come.

In the following weeks, she openly questioned my ability as a pilot to command a medical squadron to both peers and enlisted personnel. She would send e-mails on behalf of the squadron to other group commanders without informing me, causing me to be blind sided at meetings. My repeated requests to her to keep me in the loop were ignored until she ceased direct communication altogether and would exchange messages with me only through a senior enlisted go-between. This behavior undermined my authority and made it increasingly difficult to conduct squadron business. When I notified my boss about the situation, he instructed the major to "play nice." I had hoped for a stronger action, but in any event there was no change in the major's behavior.

This was a toxic environment that could not continue. My first instinct was to settle it Bronx style, but I knew that option would not be a good one for a new commander. I could demand her respect, which would just look like a pissing contest to everyone else; I could charge her with insubordination, which would be a huge distraction; or I could remove her from the squadron permanently, which would deny the squadron of this officer's valuable experience. There seemed to be no good options.

Then I came up with one. I arranged a six-week temporary assignment for the major outside the squadron but still in the medical field. This would give her a chance to demonstrate her proficiency, enjoy some recognition for her contributions, and practice leadership, not to mention making my life easier. When the major returned, she had a fresh perspective and a more positive attitude. There was less tension, more cooperation, and the squadron functioned smoothly again.

## SQUADRON COMMANDER

Squadron commander was one of my favorite positions from the leadership aspect. It was a good test of my leadership and ability to handle a wide variety of challenges. And the challenges kept coming.

One guy was violating a medical restriction and sustained an injury to avoid taking a PT test. He lied and was trying to game the system. I wrote him a letter of admonishment, less harsh than a letter of reprimand. He was in the process of moving for a transfer and his wife was pregnant at the time. Because of the letter of admonishment, the Air Force canceled his orders. He didn't take that well. His response involved taking illegal drugs and going out on the town brandishing a loaded weapon. He tried to provoke police officers so they would have to shoot him. Fortunately, he was arrested without any shooting. They took him to the hospital and flushed whatever drugs he took. They put him under surveillance for 72 hours and kept him for a week.

I saw him at the hospital before they transported him. I went with the superintendent of the squadron to make sure he was okay. Later he came back to the squadron. They took the gun away from him but he tried to get it back.

He was probably the only guy in the squadron who made me fearful. I worked late hours, six or seven in the evening, after most people had gone home. He was the kind of guy I was concerned would come to my office late at night, so I had my door closed and my windows open. He was not incredibly stable.

Within about three months he was removed for mental health reasons. He was just at a point that he could not do his job any more. I did see him a couple years later. It freaked me out. He came up to me in Houston Hobby Airport. He's like, "Hey, ma'am, how's it going?" I was looking around for the nearest cop, but it turned out fine. He was doing really well, his wife was pregnant again, his kid was doing fine, and he was glad he was out.

## BREAKING POINT

In the midst of all this, I was told that due to my impressive record as temporary squadron commander, I was being offered the job of commander at Palmdale, a military/civilian facility where Lockheed serviced U2 aircraft. But to qualify for that job, I had to get a four-ship upgrade to my T-38 instructor rating, which meant additional work on the ground and in the air.

My mom was going through chemo treatment in New York, I had been separated from my new husband for most of the first year of our marriage, and there was continuous interpersonal drama in the squadron for which I was director of operations as well as commander. Personal and professional responsibilities compounded.

I was not flying well. I was having a tough time qualifying for my four ship upgrade. I knew it was serious when I started failing flights because it's not something I normally do. I'd done well throughout flight school. I can count the number of "downs" in my career. My first check ride in my helicopter I got a down. And then in the U2 program I got a down in my first high flight because I was too comfortable in the suit. Those were the only times.

When I was doing my four ship training I failed consecutive flights. I was nauseous. I was starting to think I wasn't going to make it. I needed more time in a day. I was failing and I couldn't help myself. It was killing me. I struggled. I failed. I wouldn't say anything, I was just sucking it up.

It was one of the few times in my life that I was at the breaking point. Something was going to spill out or I was going to fall apart. Then by the grace of God or luck or my guardian angel wing man, I finally passed my check ride for the four-ship upgrade. I don't know how that happened, but it was a huge relief.

A few days later my friend Mike, commander of the 1st RS training squadron, came to me. He had previously been chief of safety, and we had deployed together. He knew I was struggling. "What the hell is going on with you? Do I need to stop your training? What is happening?"

"A week ago, that might have been the case, but I'm all right now." I hadn't told anyone about my mom, but I told him.

"We need to stop training you."

"No, I'll be fine. I'm good." A lot of pilots do that. I was worried about my mom, the people in my squadron, about my marriage, my career. I'm good at holding it all in and not letting it explode. That was one of the few times where I came close to detonation.

I'd had a huge falling out with my aunt in New York. When I had first come to visit my mom, when she had her surgery, my aunt made a comment, "Oh, the prodigal daughter returns." She called me a prima donna. She said I was never home except for once a year or two years. The irony was that New York was no longer my home. I had my own home in California, and I wasn't there all that much, either.

But I was over the top. The crisis was past, and I was headed to Palmdale.

# PALMDALE

LOCKHEED, the manufacturer of the U2, has a facility at Palmdale where they do major repairs and modifications to the aircraft. There is a civilian contingent and a military contingent. I was commander of the military detachment, the government flight representative (GFR). My job was to make sure an aircraft returned to the Air Force by Lockheed was airworthy and ready for service. The contractor would fly it, I would fly it, and if everything functioned properly, I would accept it on behalf of the Air Force.

The military/civilian relationship in Palmdale was an interesting dynamic. I oversaw the whole operation. The Air Force had maintainers, administrative personnel, and engineers because we did flight test as well. They were all under my command. The civilian personnel were not, but they had to listen to me. If the contractors damaged the aircraft, if they were negligent or didn't perform the repairs or modifications they were supposed to, I could write them up in a corrective action report. There are different consequences, known as severities, to a report like that, depending on how serious the problem is. They range from the contractor fixing the problem all the way up to the Air Force refusing to pay for the work.

The GFR has a lot of power. The contractors have to respect her and maybe even fear her because she can make their lives difficult. I didn't want to do that, but I knew the people who would be flying U2s all over the world, and these aircraft had to meet the standard. If something was done incorrectly or overlooked, I was going to call them on it.

## SCHEDULED MAINTENANCE

I flew U2s, I'd seen Air Force personnel service and maintain them, and I was interested in the process. I'd watch the Lockheed contractors working and occasionally I'd say, "Why are you doing that to this aircraft?"

Usually I'd get an answer like, "We've been doing this for 30 years, and that's how we do it." Maybe that was enough to get previous GFRs off their case, but it was not acceptable to me.

"Show me in the tech order why this procedure is being done."

This was something they were not used to hearing. When I first got there, they'd try to ignore me. They hadn't had a corrective action report in years. But when they weren't following the tech order and something broke, I wrote them up.

On one occasion, I had just accepted a U2 that had undergone a complete overhaul, called programmed depot maintenance, which is required after 6000 flight hours. They had stripped that aircraft down to the frame, updated equipment and systems, and put it back together. It had been there almost a year, and now it was fully refurbished, almost like new. I was scheduled to fly the aircraft from Palmdale back to Beale that day.

To start the U2 jet engine, we use a piece of equipment called a start cart, which is a mobile air compressor powered by a big V-8 engine. The high pressure air hose is attached to the U2 engine and the compressed air turns the turbines until they attain enough revolutions for ignition.

The manual clearly states that the hose must be attached to the aircraft before the compressor is started. I was in my office preparing for my flight when one of my maintenance guys came in with bad news.

He had watched the Lockheed contractors wheel out the start cart, unspool the hose, and switch it on without first attaching it to the aircraft. According to the Lockheed contractor, they did that to clear the debris from the hose.

If you've ever seen a fire hose unattended, you know that the force coming out of the nozzle causes that hose to flop and flail around like a cobra hit with a taser. The nozzle becomes a very dangerous tethered wrecking ball. That's why you see several firefighters holding a fire hose, because it has to be controlled.

The same thing happened with the compressed air hose. It flipped and flopped with uncontrolled force until the nozzle punched a hole in the newly refurbished U2, just under the wing, very close to the fuel bladder, which was full at the time. If it had punctured the fuel bladder, a serious mishap might have been much worse. As it was, the damage was limited to a hole in the aircraft which prevented me from flying it to Beale.


When my maintenance guy told me what happened, I was mad. I went to get the Lockheed supervisor and brought him down to the flight line to see the results of not following procedure. Then he was mad. I wrote a corrective action report, telling exactly what happened. The civilian contractors couldn't believe it, but it was their fault. Lockheed repaired the damage. Some of these guys got fired.

Not all the contractors were like that. Most of them were professional and dedicated. There were contractors at Palmdale who had been working on this aircraft for decades. They took great pride in their work. One member of the ground crew was 81 years old. He'd been with Lockheed for 60 years so he'd worked on the U2 most of his career. He was awesome. One of his jobs was to place the wheel chocks when the aircraft was stationary. He'd run with the chocks, kind of slowly. But he moved faster than some of the young guys, especially the vegans. I was more concerned about their health than his. They looked like they might not make it.

## MAINTAINING SCHEDULE

There was a new Lockheed guy in our building, a millennial named Jason. He thought he could just drop by my office at any time and chat without an appointment. I'd be on the phone or involved in some important business and he'd just barge in past my secretary and plant himself in my office. He was a pain. After one poorly-timed interruption, I snapped at him and he went back to his hole whimpering.

A week later, Jason came back to me and said, "You know, Merryl, you really shouldn't yell at me."

I stopped what I was doing to have one last unscheduled meeting with him. "If you don't like me yelling at you, get the fuck out of my office. How dare you come in here?"

He was shocked. Whatever it took for him to come in there, he was not expecting that answer. I crushed his spirit. But if you come into my office unannounced, bypass my secretary, and interrupt whenever you want, that's on you. You're coming into the lion's den. If you don't want to get yelled at, don't mess with the lion. Come through proper channels. So he never did that again.

My boss when I was at Palmdale was an officer at Robins AFB in Georgia. But our facility was technically under the administration of Edwards AFB which was just a few miles from us. One day I got a call from Edwards. A 19 year-old airman at FE Warren Air Base in Wyoming had taken his own life with a handgun. The officer from Edwards said, "You gotta go tell a family that their son just killed himself."

I didn't know the son, I didn't know the family, and all this happened over a thousand miles from me. But the young man's family lived in Southern California, and notifications of this kind are handled in person. So I took a chaplain, a chief and a medic for a two hour car ride to deliver the news. We found the house and knocked on the door, but no one was home. We took a break, got some coffee, and came back. This time the mother answered. Seeing a bunch of uniforms on the front porch is never a good sign for a military family. I told the airman's mother what had happened, since I was the senior officer present. There's no easy way to do it, but that's another responsibility of command. It's part of the job.

## GET IT DONE

When I was done with my command job at Palmdale I was looking for a joint service job. The Air Force assignments guy told me, "We don't know where we're going to put you. But it probably won't be a joint job because you're not a school select." School select was an officer chosen to attend the Professional Military Education course. But in order to qualify for PME, I needed a joint service job - a position where I worked with more than one service. I was getting the runaround. I called Delgetti again. "Dude, I need some help." We knew a lot of the same people, but he knew them better.

Delgetti called a couple of admirals and the admirals got me in touch with a retired Air Force two-star. We talked quite a bit. He gave me the name of another gentleman who worked in DC and I interviewed with him. He was part of an admirals group and I was on the e-mail chain. There was a retired two-star, or three-star, a black officer, who invited me to reach out to him.

• • •

The retired general got me in contact with an active duty flag rank officer in DC. When I talked to him on the phone, I immediately knew by the way he talked that he was from the Tri-State area. "Sir, where are you from?"

"I'm from Massachusetts."

"Aw, man. Please don't tell me you're a Red Sox fan."

"Why, you a Yankees fan?"

"Heck, yeah I am."

There was silence on the phone. I thought that I had probably just killed the whole thing. Then he said, "Yeah, I would love for you to come work with my organization. I'll put a by-name request in for you."

He went to the Air Force Personnel Center to do a by-name request (very unusual), and AFPC said they had already cut my orders. Those orders came through and said I was going to NORAD /Northcom in Colorado Springs for a joint staff position, the job I originally wanted.

When I got those orders, I was excited. All my assignments had been overseas. Now I would be in North American air defense, working on policy. I was going to get my joint staff ticket punched. For promotion purposes, it looked good on a resume. Most people in the U2 community go to the Air Force staff, not the joint staff. Joint staff encompasses all military services. I had served in two branches. I spoke Navy and I spoke Air Force. I was well-suited to the job. I'd done a command tour and a DO tour. The timing was ideal.

I do not know to this day if it was because of Delgetti, or the influence of the star-studded network, or if the Air Force already had plans for me. But I know I had been outside the pipeline. People had forgotten where I was. I tapped into my network and discovered a lot of people who went out of their way to help me. It's about being proactive and reaching out to the people you know.

I was long enough in the game to know you can't just hope that you advance. Hope is not a career strategy. You've gotta get it done. Make sure you have all the forces working for you. Use all your resources.

## 19

# TWO BECOME THREE

When we got married, Kjell wanted two children, I wanted zero. I compromised. "Okay, we'll do one." If you think about it, though, the difference between having one child and having two is much less than the difference between having one child and having none at all. So maybe I surrendered a little more territory.

Having a child means you can't be selfish. When Kjell and I were married, it was just us, life was good. Kids require all your time, they're soul suckers of life. But it's fun. It's fine.

And it's not just like having a cat, which I have had since OCS. Cats get up at four in the morning and walk on your face and do the whole "meow, meow" bit. And then I have to say, "Dude, go back to sleep, or I'm putting you on the menu." And then a smart cat will quiet down.

With my deployments, Kjell and I were living apart again. He had reached the point where he was okay not having any kids. There was no room for kids in our lives. Since I was a U2 pilot, that seemed sensible. Flying at high altitude in a pressure suit isn't usually recommended for expectant mothers.

But by the time I got to Colorado Springs, I was cool with the idea of becoming a parent. Fine, let's do this. But now Kjell wasn't so sure it was the right time.

"Bro, it's never the right time." But now the guy who originally wanted two kids wasn't sure he wanted any.

I was 41 at the time. I believed there was no way I was going to get pregnant–surely those days were behind me. So I told Kjell, "In about ten minutes, I'm gonna be naked in the other room. The ball's in your court."

The fun part is trying. We were living apart, not seeing each other very often, but when we got together, it was on like Donkey Kong. I'd get drunk and then say, "Let's go." A lot of people try to plan everything. I just took it in stride. People get too caught up in the process, like it has to fit in this bubble. You set yourself up for disappointment having all these detailed expectations. Just go with the flow, have fun with it. If it happens, it happens.

Five months later, I was in Vegas where I was going to meet my mom for the weekend. I got to the hotel room and I was going to have a drink, and I felt sick to my stomach. That doesn't happen that often. Why don't I feel well? The wheels started turning. I thought, just in case, I better stop drinking. I didn't drink the rest of the trip.

When I got back to Colorado I started eating weird things; hard-boiled eggs with salt and vinegar potato chips. One of the contractors I worked with was Rick. He's a very quiet man, very religious. He did top quality work. There are some people you just immediately bond with. Rick was one of those. We hit if off well. I was having lunch with him one day. He saw my bizarre meal and just smiled. I said, "Bro, don't even say it."

My job at NORAD/NorthCom was a joint billet. I wanted to qualify as a Joint Staff Officer, which is an officer who has worked with multiple service branches. To get that qualification, I had to be at NORAD/NorthCom for thirty-six months and take the joint professional military education course (JPME). JPME is a set of courses to prepare officers in all branches for high level military leadership. It's a requirement to be a general, although not necessarily a colonel. At first they weren't going to send me, but I kept pressing until they approved my request. I didn't want to miss this opportunity, and I wasn't going to let a pregnancy get in the way. My staff tour wouldn't involve flying–the timing was perfect.

I drove out to Virginia for the JPME course, taking the cats with me. Three days later, I get a pregnancy test. Sure enough, the test comes back positive. I was like, "Damn, I'm pregnant. All right. Cool."

The first person I called was Rick. He was excited, but not surprised. Then I called Dr. Croach. Marilyn Croach wasn't my doctor, but she worked in the building where I worked. She's a very charismatic senior executive service officer, the civilian equivalent of a one-star, who has had a stellar career. I would stop by her office and talk with her when she was free. I was always fascinated by her perspective on stuff. Some one once described me as a force of nature. Dr. Croach is a force of nature, but she's quiet. She's more refined, like a Southern lady. She'll still tell you that you're doing a lousy job, but she'll say it really nicely. She'll serve that turd with flowers and you'll be so grateful to accept it because of her presentation. When I told her, she was really happy for me.

Kjell was next, so at least he was in the top three. My husband is an interesting man. He has his own career and his own life. He's ambitious, he wants to succeed in a lot of things. He knows I can take a lot of stuff. He knows he can go deploy and do things, and I'll be fine. If there's a conflict between doing a first ultrasound or going TDY for reserve duty, he knows I can take care of that. Even before I got pregnant, he told me, "I can't be there for everything." I got my first ultrasound while I was in JPME. Kjell wasn't there for the first one. Obviously I didn't like that.

I didn't want to tell anyone. I didn't want to get too excited. There are so many things that can happen. People would say they were pregnant, then have a miscarriage, and it's really awkward. I didn't want to put people in that situation. An Egyptian student in the JPME class who knew I was pregnant would tell me every time I was on the treadmill, "You shouldn't be doing this."

I knew my child was going to be a boy in the first trimester. I coerced the nurse to tell me at my first appointment at 8 weeks. She didn't want to say, but I kept asking, "Boy or girl?"

"I can't tell you anything."

I had to work on her. "Come on, how long have you been doing this? Thirty years? You've seen a lot of penises and vaginas. Are you saying you can't tell?"

So she goes through this whole routine. "Here's the head, here's the legs, and here's a little bump here, not sure what it is." So I got it, I knew what she was saying. I was relieved it was a boy. If there was another girl in the house with me, we'd have two queens in the house, or a queen and a princess, and that doesn't work.

At that point I was thinking, "This is a potential child." I mean, anything could happen. I'll believe it when I see it. I called him "fetus" up until the day he was born. Not that there wasn't a maternal attachment. But I'd show up at the doctor's office and say, "How is the fetus doing?"

The doctor laughed at me. "That's a very technical term." I had zero expectations going in. I was nauseous but I wasn't throwing up. Second trimester was better. Second trimester I'd eat a Big Mac and vanilla shake and fries with no salt–I would crush those. By the third trimester I was huge.

I was working the whole time, and the fetus was active when I was asleep, which was annoying. I'd get to work and I'd be pissed because I hadn't slept. Finally, I decided two could play this game. I'd get to work and play techno music as loud as can be and I'd put the speaker against my stomach and say, "Wake up!" I'd just screw with him the whole time. If he kept me up all night, I'd rock his world all day.

Overall it was an easy pregnancy. I was at Fort Carson hospital in Colorado for the delivery. The worst part was that the nurse who gave me the IV missed the vein. My blood pressure was elevated so I never dilated to 10 centimeters. After 18 hours of labor, my civilian doctor told me he was going off shift. He could do a C-section or he'd hand it off to the next doctor in rotation.

I knew the next doctor who was coming in. I had seen her once during my pregnancy. She was a military doctor. We got in an argument about the medication I was taking. She kept going on about standard procedures and I was trying to tell her about what I wanted and she wouldn't listen. And I outranked her!

So I said, "We're done with this exam." I found a new doctor, a civilian. He was reading my file and found a note from the previous doctor. It said, "She's difficult." So he was wary at first.

I told him what happened, and then I said, "If she comes into the delivery room at any time, I will get up, no matter how dilated I am, and I will walk out. I'm not even playing with you. I don't want her anywhere around me or my kid. I will go to blows with her."

So when he told me she was coming on, I said, "Let's do the C section."

She came in the room while I was getting prepped. "How are you doing?"

"Good."

Then she left.

I had an epidural along with some other medications. It wasn't as good as the morphine drip, but I was feeling no pain. The anasthesiologist was there, adjusting the dosage. I told him, "That is a great epidural."

He was a military doctor also. He said, "Ma'am, your breasts are exposed. Do you want me to cover those up?"

"Dude, my vagina is hanging out in front of all you clowns. Do you think I care what else you see?" He cracked up and everybody else started laughing. Then I sort of chuckled.

"Ma'am, are you okay?"

"Yeah, I just farted. Does it smell?"

Everybody cracked up again and the doctor had to step back to compose himself. "I can't take this," he said, shaking his head. Everybody was having a good time.


My son was 22 inches, 8 pounds, 2 ounces. Almost two feet tall. He was long, not fat.

I was frustrated because it took them a long time to give him to me. I was impatient. "Hey, I'm the mother, give me my baby."

They brought him over all gift wrapped. He was pretty pale. Is this white child really mine? "He's really light. I hope he darkens up a little."

I wasn't crying or anything. I didn't hear trumpets blaring like in *The Lion King*. I was drugged up, I was exposed. I was just thinking, "Cool." And also, "I'm glad that shit is over."


Flynn Obari Tengesdal was born on November 20th, 2012. Tengesdal is half Norwegian, half Irish. Flynn is an Irish name - it was going to be Flynn or Tristan. His middle name, Obari, is a Nigerian name that means "mighty." Kjell picked that. Flynn is my little black Irish Viking.

Kjell took a year of paternity leave to take care of Flynn while I worked. That was awesome. I love the fact that he took a year off. But he was still an engineering duty officer in the reserves, he earned his jump wings (at the age of 47), and he was doing his college work. When you have a newborn, it's a joint effort. It's very frustrating when you come home and hear, "He wouldn't go to sleep and I couldn't get my work done." But it was awesome he took a year off.

## BACK TO WORK

In December of 2013, I reported back to Beale. Flynn was 13 months old. I went back to Beale as deputy operations group commander. Three days before Flynn's second birthday, I received a 365 day non-voluntary deployment order. I had not done a deployment like that in ten years, since I'd been in the Air Force. The only way to avoid that deployment would be to retire from the Air Force. I already had more than twenty years in military service, so that would be a considerable sacrifice.

I was a lieutenant colonel and my review board for colonel had not met yet. The Air Force gives you a performance recommendation form (PRF). In that PRF, your boss and boss's boss review your career and write your performance review. In the summary there are three boxes Definitely Promote, Promote and Do Not Promote. If you get the first one, your odds of getting the promotion are about 90%. If you get a Promote, your odds are even or a little worse - say between 30% and 50%. No need to tell you what "Do Not Promote" means.

My PRF came after I'd been in my job a very short time. I got the "Promote" rating. This came with an offer for a lateral transfer to wing inspector general, reporting to the wing commander. It did not look like an advance of any kind.

When I got the 365, a lot of heavy things were going on. Outside, it all looked routine, but inside it didn't feel that way. I had three days to decide. The vice wing commander hand-delivered the orders and it felt like he was saying, "Haha, sucker." I thought I was getting fired from my current position as group deputy operations commander. I got what I considered a lackluster PRF. It seemed like the military didn't want me.

I turned down the inspector job on my son's second birthday. I figured he needed me more than the Air Force did.

I went to my boss, Col. Douglas Lee, the wing commander, who was just back from a temporary duty assignment. We had known each other previously. I walked up and said, "Sir, I just turned down a 365 so I'll be retiring at the end of the year." His face got red. He didn't know what to say. He was clearly upset.

"Can I talk you out of it?"

"Sir, I've already submitted the paperwork."

"I didn't know about this."

I believed him, but I also told him, "Your vice wing commander knew about it because he hand-delivered the orders to me. Your ops group commander knew because it originated in his office." I told him I'd stay in my current job until it was time for me to go.

When things are going on in the wing commander's office that he doesn't know about, he gets pissed. I imagine there was some major ass chewing going on because the operations commander showed up at my office. He was acting weird, even for a guy who was already pretty weird. He said he was really sorry I turned down this new position.

I'd told the wing commander that I would stay until my retirement in 2016, so that's what I did. February of 2015, the list was coming out for colonel. I knew my name wasn't going to be on that list. I almost didn't go to work that day. I didn't want to hear, "Aw, sorry you didn't make it," a few dozen times from everybody at work. I drove to the base blasting Rage Against the Machine and pounding on the steering wheel. I got to the gate and I almost turned my car around and went home. But I had a photo shoot scheduled to go with an article the Air Force had just done about me.

· · ·

I was in the physiological support office getting integrated into the pressure suit when Col. Lee and the chief of the base came in. Col. Lee said, "Merryl, we've been looking for you."

I was showing no emotion, but I didn't know how long I could hold it together. "Sir, I've been very busy."

"I just wanted to congratulate you."

What kind of bullshit was this? Congratulate me for what? Was there some sort of consolation prize, some Miss Congeniality award for not making colonel? "Sir, what are you talking about?"

"You made colonel." Then he pulled out a bottle of champagne, shook my hand and pulled me close. "Now you really have a decision to make, whether you're going to stay or not."

I was one of three or four people on the base who made colonel. Once I got that promotion, all the people who had been treating me like crap started changing their tunes. I hadn't changed, but there's reverence for the rank. People started explaining why they mistreated me when they didn't have to. And I'd just think, "Hmmmm."

When you become a colonel, you move to the colonel's group. They take care of all your stuff. I still had the 365 over my head. The Air Force said they were going to change my assignment to something else in Afghanistan. And I said my answer remained the same. I would not take the orders. I asked them for family accompany orders to Turkey, or Iran, or Korea, or almost anyplace else. I'd do it for two years. They said no. It was business for them, personal for me.

## SAYING NO TO SPIELBERG

Saying no was getting to be a habit, but I never anticipated the next chance I had to say it. In 2015, Steven Spielberg was making a movie called *Bridge of Spies* about the 1962 exchange of a Soviet spy for Francis Gary Powers, the American pilot of the first U2 to be shot down. The production company came to Beale to shoot footage of U2s.

Part of our cooperation with the production was to give Spielberg a close-up view of U2 landing procedures. So I invited him to join me in a mobile chase car, in this case a high performance Camaro, and watch one of our pilots who was doing touch-and-gos for the movie cameras.

Spielberg was a nice guy. His father had been a B-25 radio operator in the 490th Bomb Squadron in India during World War II. He was interested in all the aircraft, procedures and history.

I was not just Spielberg's driver, but one of two mobiles that day. The camera crew was in the other chase car and Spielberg was in mine. There was a problem with the camera, so the camera car had to go back so the technicians could get the camera working. This left me as the only mobile for the aircraft doing the landing rotations.

Spielberg must have figured he'd seen enough, so he said, "I'll just get out now."

That's when I said something to Spielberg that he's probably not used to hearing. "No, you can't do that."

There followed an uncomfortable silence that lasted at least a minute. But I couldn't let him walk across an active runway with aircraft doing touch-and-gos and chase cars driving at 100 miles-an-hour, back and forth.

The other mobile pulled up with the camera now operating, and radioed to me, "Two to chase." So we were set up to get the shot of the landing U2 from the point of view of the mobile, driving 100 miles per hour right behind the aircraft. Both mobiles took off to match the speed of the incoming U2 and got right on his tail. We got the shot.

Spielberg was jubilant. "That was awesome!" He repeated it a few times for emphasis. He was totally jazzed. We got back to the hangar and he jumped out, describing the pedal-to-the-medal ride down the runway to the rest of the crew in very excited terms. That was my last brush with show business until *Tough as Nails*.

# RETIREMENT

*If I can't drink a beer with you at the end of the workday, someone took it personal. We need to fix that before the next workday.*

IN AUGUST 2015, I was all set to retire. Col. Lee said his boss, General Jack Shanahan, commander of the 25th Air Force, wanted to talk to me. About what? Was this about my inspector general job. "No," he said. "It's about you."

I talked to some people to find out why General Shanahan might want to talk to me. The Air Force only had two rated pilots who were black females at the O6 (Air Force colonel) level–me and General Stayce Harris (the first black female three-star in the Air Force). So I went to talk to her, and she referred me to a colleague of hers. His advice was just to tell General Shanahan my story.

I met with General Shanahan and I told him I wasn't looking for any favors, but I wasn't going to change my decision, because my two year old needed his mom. We talked on a secure line for more than half an hour. I told him my story. At the end it was like a scene from *The Godfather*. He said, "I don't know if I can do anything. If you haven't heard from me by December, go ahead and retire. But we'll be in touch."

Next day I'm in my wing commander's office. He says "I'm going to show you this, but I never showed you this." He prints out Shanahan's email to the chief of staff of the Air Force, a four star, about why they should retain me. "Why is she retiring? Is there anything we can do for this officer?"

The answer was, "We can get her to DC."

The great thing was that General Shanahan believes in diversity. He did some research and he went to bat for me. He ended up at the Pentagon and he was my mentor when I was there. He went out on a limb for me. He was happy I stayed in longer.

When I went to the Pentagon I was director of inspections, working under the Inspector General, Lt. General Gregory Biscone. There was also a deputy IG who was very political. He knew a lot of people. On occasion, General Shanahan would invite me to lunch in the executive lounge, reserved for generals and their equivalents. Every time we'd go, the Deputy IG would see us and have this look on his face like, "Why are you in here? Why are you having lunch with General Shanahan? Who else do you know?" You could tell not knowing was killing him inside. It tickled me no end.

If I saw the Deputy IG, I'd always be pleasant. "Hello, Sir, how are you?" I'd just fuck with him. I'd have lunch with a navy admiral, and the deputy IG was totally perplexed. He couldn't figure out how I knew these people. At the Pentagon, you had to have some sort of sponsorship to survive. If you're truly playing the game in there, someone has to have your back. It allows you to network, it allows you to force people's hands if you need to.

People are more cautious if you have a mentor, or even if they think you have a mentor. When I was there with Gen. Shanahan, we'd just be having a conversation, talking about Elon Musk or something. But the people watching us had no idea what we were talking about. And that made them cautious.

## "-*ING*" WORDS

General Biscone was a good boss. He didn't tolerate anything substandard. I was sitting in a meeting with him one time. It was General Biscone, the Deputy IG, me, and maybe a dozen other people in the room. We were in a teleconference with the Air Force inspection agency.

General Biscone turned to me and asked, "Merryl, what's your office got?"

I talked about the different inspection projects that were going on. We were working on this, we were waiting for that, we were expecting something else.

General Biscone was a short Italian guy, but his stars made him taller. He looked at me and took off his glasses and I knew something bad was coming. I thought, "Shit, what did I do?"

"Merryl, I hear a lot of -*ing* words. Working on this, working on that. Do you know what -*ing* words mean to me? They mean you're not doing shit and not producing results." I couldn't believe it. He was calling me out in front of all these people. He was very nice and cordial about it but at that level it was an ass chewing.

Then I realized what he was saying. "Stop telling me what you're doing and show me results." He was teaching me. It was one of those moments, "I'm going to school you, young Obi-Wan, about what I expect." It was a rookie move on my part. I should have known better. I was playing at a different level and I should have been prepared.

"Sir, I read you loud and clear. I'll get back to you with exact dates and progress reports." And I did. He didn't know me well enough to understand that when I said I was working on it, that I really was working on it. I was moving the ball. But he was going to have to report to the Secretary of the Air Force, and telling the top man, "Don't worry, Merryl is working on it," just wasn't going to fly. The Secretary of the Air Force would want hard facts, and that's what Gen. Biscone wanted from me.

. . .

Now when people tell me, "Hey, Merryl, I'm working on it," it's unsatisfactory.

My response is, "I hear a lot of *-ing* words. But what are you producing? What's the end game? If this thing doesn't happen, what's the next step?" I learned that from Gen. Biscone.

## THE AFTER EFFECTS

I flew the U2 from 2004 to 2010. High altitude flying puts a lot of stress on the body. When I was flying, the cabin was pressurized to the equivalent of 29,500 feet--the same altitude as at the top of Mount Everest--for hours at a time, breathing 100% oxygen. At 70,000 feet the pilot also does not have all of Earth's atmosphere to filter out harmful radiation. U2 pilots experience decompression issues, hypoxia, and brain lesions.

A brain lesion is tissue damage to the brain from injury or disease. Symptoms range from nausea, lack of appetite and vision issues to memory loss, impaired cognitive ability and seizures. I left the military with twenty brain lesions. Usually you start getting those in your 60s. U2 pilots and mountain climbers get them a little earlier.

When I was flying there was a rash of people experiencing symptoms consistent with those from concussion injuries. I had a friend in his mid-thirties who was driving to work and had to pull over because he forgot where he was going. Another friend came back from deployment with short term memory loss and inability to complete a sentence. In 2012 we had one guy get decompressions sickness six hours into the flight. He inflated the suit, which is the prescribed procedure, and that alleviated his symptoms. But he kept flying and the symptoms returned, only they were more severe. He threw up in his helmet, suffered from hypoxia, and his whole central nervous system was compromised. He finally got back to the field, almost crashed between two hangars, and finally landed and collapsed over the yoke. They rushed him to a decompression chamber as he was going into circulatory collapse. He recovered and survived, but for a while he would still forget things like how to shave. He was finally cleared to fly again, had another incident, and that was it–he stopped flying. He had suffered permanent brain damage.

At first the Air Force thought these symptoms were caused by the stress of the demanding deployment schedule–60 days on, 60 days off. They now believe all these problems were due to brain lesions caused by decompression sickness (DCS). In 2015 they redesigned the cockpit to bring the cabin pressure down to 15,000 feet. Pilots don't experience those symptoms any more. Just the older pilots, such as myself. The only reason I know I have twenty lesions is that I was part of a 2013 Air Force study of U2 pilots. I just wanted to have an MRI to make sure I wasn't going to have an aneurism, so I volunteered for the study. It was a free scan, why not? They scanned us and gave us cognitive tests to check our IQs.

It turns out twenty brain lesions is not excessive. Some pilots had as many as one hundred. We don't know what the long term effects are. It's like going to space--your body undergoes physiological changes such as loss of bone density. When you resign or retire from the military, you go through an exit medical appointment at the VA to see if you qualify for any percentage of disability. If they do find any disability, you have to prove to the military that it was caused while in the line of service. I couldn't prove my brain lesions were caused by flying because there was no baseline. I didn't have a brain scan prior to my service, so the lesions could have been there the whole time. It's doubtful, but that's the way the system works. They denied my claim for disability.

•　•　•

I don't think they realized how bad it could be for certain pilots. That's why they invested the money to change the cabin pressure for the U2. When I stopped flying and went to NORAD/Northcom, I realized after several months that I was seeing and thinking more clearly. It's not that I couldn't think before, but it had taken more effort. I felt like I was emerging from a fog.

A year before I went to the Pentagon, the pain in my hip was getting intense. Just walking to the aircraft with my parachute was excruciating. Once I was seated in the aircraft, the pain was gone, so I flew. I didn't tell the flight doc. In the military you don't tell doctors anything. It's a reason for them to disqualify you. (The military took care of my hip replacement after I retired.) You talk to any pilot who always dreamed of flying, she's not going to let a little sniffle or muscle cramp end her career. Even when I had frostbite, my attitude was, "Put me in, coach."

On the other hand, as a commander, if one of my pilots was impaired, I'd pull him aside and we'd have a talk. I did that once when I was the commander at Palmdale and there was a civilian Lockheed engineer, a former U2 pilot who no longer flew, who drove a chase car for us. He was in his 60s and he started manifesting some things I'd notice when I was in the car with him. He couldn't click the radio button because his arthritis was so bad. He couldn't write with his right hand so he'd have to write with his left hand. He started forgetting a lot of things and I was watching this very rapid decline in his mental capacity.

One of the other civilian pilots I spoke to about him said he was fine. I said, "Naw, Dude, you gotta remove him." I felt bad because he was a fellow U2 pilot, he was a brother. I had to talk to the guy who was in charge of the engineers. "You've gotta put him in another job. He can't mobile any more. He's a danger." I felt bad about it but I had to make a decision.

No one's trying to cover up. Professionals suck it up, they do what they need to do to finish the mission. I was riding with one pilot who was a mobile, a veteran officer. He was feeling sick. He said, "Merryl, I need you to take my flight." He just couldn't fly that day and he knew it. I took his flight and it was the right thing to do all around.

Reducing the cabin altitude in the U2 was a major improvement. When I flew subsequent aircraft with that modification, I could feel the difference. I wasn't as tired the next day. The military doesn't take unnecessary risks. They weigh the risk against the reward. They know there are some long term effects of flying at high altitude. The information that is received from these pilots putting their bodies through extraordinary physiological stress is worth the risk. The U2 obtains important data that can save lives. One U2 mission can help tens or hundreds of people.

You think about the *Challenger*. Is it worth the risk of going into space, or going to Mars or all the other things they have planned? Yes. You delegate the decision down to the individual. You can opt out if you want to. A commander has the authority to intercede if he thinks a pilot can't do his job. But we don't want to be micromanaged. I know the risks. Let me do my job.

Military people have this underlying feeling that we're in it to win it. There's an understanding among us that we're going to get the mission done. It's different at the Pentagon because they write procedures and policies and publications. The troops on the line see these things come out and they think, "Oh, you jack-asses, you don't know what it's like to fly the mission." Actually, they do know, but they're coming from a place of reason. When you're at the tactical level, the rules can seem needlessly restrictive. So you think, "Fuck you guys, you're in the Pentagon in your zero knot chair, you don't know what you're doing." But they do know. They're just trying to establish policy that is beneficial for everyone. I've seen it from both sides.

Being a military pilot opened a lot of doors for me. I was able to do things and go places and meet people I never would have in any other career. When I started at the Pentagon in October 2015, I was working at the center of the United States military, working with people at the peaks of their careers. If I stayed in, I could have gone further. But I knew my time in uniform was coming to an end. I hadn't joined the military to be a general, to rise as high as I could in rank.

There are people who are highly motivated and hard working who achieve what they want and then move the goal post so that they still have something lofty to aspire to. That could have been me. I could have stayed in to see if I could make general. Then I could have stayed to see if I could get that second star. But what would I gain by that, other than more money and a nicer office?

None of it would be as cool as going to my son's soccer game or watching him grow. My mom worked hard and sacrificed to give me a better life. I wanted to spend time with my son like my mom spent with me. I retired from the military in November 2017.

Part Four

# THE NEXT MISSION

# MY RETIREMENT CEREMONY

LOTS OF PEOPLE showed up for my retirement ceremony at the Military Women's Memorial in Arlington. It's an inspiring monument and it was great to have family and friends there. My friend Sri came, my cousin who works at the Pentagon was there with her kids, lots of Navy and Air Force people I had served with–Ronnie Robinson, General Rock, and General Stayce Harris, who presided over the ceremony. At the end, I was exhausted. Retirements are highly emotional, but I didn't cry, so it was good.

Afterward, Sri came with me to Arlington National Cemetery. My mom and Kjell's mom had each given me a bouquet of roses. I took a rose from each bouquet. I left one at Eric Cranford's stone, my friend from the helo squadron who died at the Pentagon on 9/11. The other rose, I left for "Muff", Dwayne Dively, who died in a U2 crash in 2005 when I was on my way to Korea. It was a gray, rainy day, made better because I got to pay my respects to my friends.

Sri visited the stone of her great uncle twice removed, a World War II vet. We started talking about the recent election and got into a pretty heated political debate. It seems that happens more and more. People have always disagreed about politics, but there seems to be less tolerance for differing opinions than there used to be.

What I love about the United States is that you can like whoever you want. People are so left, so right. We need to get back to center. People get too caught up with Republican or Democrat; these people are taking my jobs, those people are making too much money. Just shut your pie hole and do your work. Stop complaining.

## THE PRICE OF FREEDOM

We, in the military, defend other people's freedom. But, to do that, we give up some of our own. We have to conform to a particular way of life, follow a strict set of rules. We all make that choice freely. We give our all. In return, we are allowed to be Americans and live in the freest society on this earth.

I joined the military with the goal of becoming an astronaut, but even if I hadn't been able to become a pilot, I would have joined anyway. I got a t-shirt at OCS with an American flag on the front and a slogan that said, "We give our all, she gives us her colors." That was in 1994, and I still believe the freedom we have in the United States is worth defending.

Being free doesn't mean you get everything for free. In a free society, you can make decisions, whether you want to stay in the Bronx, whether you want to leave, whether you want to get an education, or just sit on the couch all day collecting whatever subsidies you are eligible for. Within a free society are those who have and those who have not. Some of it is due to situations you're born into and can't change, but a lot of it is due to choice and that's what freedom means - it allows you to choose.

• • •

Serving in the military is a choice we all make. We don't think twice about it. We don't think anybody owes us something. All we ask in return is to see that flag flying. We would all do it again in a heartbeat. Some of my fellow pilots have made the ultimate sacrifice.

I think everyone should join the military, like in Israel, where everyone serves in the army for a few years. You get an appreciation for the military and what it stands for. You see other countries, you meet people from other parts of the world, you learn what poor is really like and get an appreciation for the freedoms you have.

The military isn't perfect. I'm not ignorant about it. The Air Force still struggles with diversity in leadership, especially in senior enlisted ranks. When I was at the Pentagon, I was one of two black female rated pilots - myself and General Harris. And, I was a transplant from the Navy. Is the Air Force really serious about diversity, or are they just paying lip service with a lot of *"ing"* words?

## OBSTACLES TO LEADERSHIP

Women face obstacles to leadership. As women get older, they want to have families and settle down. They prioritize differently. That can stunt their careers in any industry, including the military. A man knows his first priority is his career. A woman is constantly torn between career and family. I know a lot of women who stay in the military, have kids, and six months later they're deploying. That's crazy. Deploying with a newborn? I know one senior master sergeant who did that. She has some regrets.

·  ·  ·

You make sacrifices in the military. Some people are not willing to do that. They may have served twenty years and struggle to maintain some sort of work-life balance the whole time.

I don't believe there is balance. It's all controlled chaos. If you're a woman and want to make colonel or general, you have to be able to deploy at the drop of a hat. It would be hard for a single mom to do that. Women with multiple kids may go into the reserves instead. Or, maybe they don't stay late at work, just go home when it's time to go home and not worry about how that impacts their performance reports. Military women make those choices. I was given the choice of a 365 to Afghanistan, or to be at home with my son. I made the choice that my son needed me more than the Air Force. That was my decision and I was good with it.

Even in the military a person has choices. If a woman declines a job because of family needs, her boss can understand and help her out. Or, he can be butt hurt about it and put her in a penalty box. What I liked about my last two years is that I could help people, guide people, mentor people. I was in a position that I could understand problems. You don't have to get pissed off at a subordinate who doesn't make the choice that's best for you. Especially if that person is good at her job.

There's a saying "You don't bury wounded soldiers."

If something difficult is going on in a subordinate's life, you don't dismiss that person. You figure out how to help her make a contribution and shine in some other way. That's what a leader does.

## BOSS LADY

My friend Heather Fox, who became wing commander at Beale last year, is one of those amazing military women. She's up-and-coming, and she's good. She's married to a former U2 pilot, has three kids, and one grandkid. We overlapped at the Pentagon.

She was a speech writer for General Dunford, head of the Joint Chiefs of Staff. She'll be a general if she decides to stay.

I told her the only thing I wish I'd seen was how we would have worked together if I had stayed. We would have been peers, maybe I'd be vice wing commander under her. We would have got stuff done in a professional way. But when the doors were closed we'd be sitting back, taking the bras off, being ourselves, being candid. We would have had good rapport, no matter who was in charge. I think she's similar to me - hands off unless she has to be. Heather is more polished in the way she talks about things; she does things with finesse. I'm more of a hammer. It would have been fun to work with her again.

There was a small gathering at Heather's house when she made wing commander. There was another female U2 pilot there besides me and Heather, named Sarah. We separated from the guys and had girl talk for a little bit. Sarah has a daughter Flynn's age. She told us that after meeting Heather, her daughter said, "When I grow up, I want to be a boss lady." Heather was taken aback. She hadn't really seen herself as a role model.

After Sarah left, I told her, "Hey, you're going to hear that a lot. Just go with it. Don't overthink it." Not that she needs my advice. She's comfortable being the person she is - an inspiring leader.

## THE MILITARY IS A FAMILY

There's an unwritten code in the military - when you see a military family struggling, you reach out to help.

I work out with a guy named Parker whose wife is in the military. I give him a hard time because he's the dependent, and he's the guy. His wife is pregnant, they're from Georgia, and they have no family out here. So, I reached out to him, in the way that military family does. I asked him, "Dude, what's your registry? Do you need help? What do you need?" Military families are like that. He always says, "No, we don't need that." Military families have a network that spans all branches. The Navy is the same way. There's definitely more of an understanding between military people, active duty, retired, separated, prior service. We can talk raunchy, curse, be very blunt with people. There's a camaraderie there, an understanding of who we are. Sometimes it's good to be around people like that. It's hard dealing with civilians sometimes. They don't understand.

# FAMILY LIFE

MY PROBLEM NOW, is I'm retired from the military. I've been out three years. I live in a community of hardworking people - teachers, doctors, lawyers. They like the area for the quality of the education system and they have high expectations for their children. But conversations I have with civilian parents can seem inconsequential.

"Oh, my kid's going to school next year and I don't know what college she's going to, and what's the budget for the school district."

I just look at them and think; *If you only knew for a second what military people are sacrificing to protect your freedom to talk this nonsense.*

It's hard sometimes. I don't say anything because they wouldn't understand.

When I drop off my son at school, I don't spend a lot of time socializing. In the Bronx, if you look approachable, someone will approach you, usually with bad intentions. Your expression has to say; *You get any closer and I'm gonna rip your throat out.*

You have to have a thousand-yard stare, you don't smile. Most people, when they meet me, say I'm standoffish. Probably. I don't want people coming up to me.

At my son's school, parents will ask, "Oh Merryl, come help us with our Girl Scouts."

"No, I can't help you with your Girl Scouts."

Or, "Oh, Merryl, can you do this for the kids' art project?"

"No."

"Why not?"

"Because I'm disinterested." Then I walk away. I've got things to do. I'm not wrapped up in my eight year-old's life like this.

## MAKING FRIENDS

I'm attracted to people who are comfortable with themselves. When I see a foundation of honesty and goodness at a person's core, that attracts me. I met my friend Sandy in a kick boxing class. We were finishing up a workout, doing reach-throughs. This is where you stand with feet apart and you bend down and reach back behind your ankles. We were both doing this exercise. I saw her going faster, so I went faster, then she went faster and it became a competition. When we were done, we were both breathing hard. She looked at me and said, "I don't know who you are, but we're going to be friends." And we are.

There are a few parents I talk to. One mom works at the wildlife refuge. Her husband had a traumatic brain injury from a motor-cycle accident. The first time we met, she came up all sunshine and lollipops. "Hi! My name is Krista!"

I was very subdued. "I'm Merryl, mother of Flynn." Nothing more. She thought I wanted nothing to do with her, so she backed off. The next week, I saw her again. "Hey, Krista." She was surprised I remembered her name. After that, we started talking.

I observed her with her twins. She didn't baby them, she talked to them like little human beings. "Hey, stop, why are you crying?" She just seems real to me. She's cool.

Whenever I walk into an environment I start classifying people right away, based on first impressions. I go down the list; *This one's a traditional homemaker. That one's a pain in the ass. This guy thinks he's an alpha but isn't. She may be cool. There's an asshole. This lady is a hot mess. That guy's at the wrong party.*

Then I come back the next week and go down the list again. "Confirm, confirm, reevaluate, confirm."

## THE NEXT GENERATION

My son Flynn likes scary stuff. Maybe it's hereditary–all the D&D mementos from my youth. We have gnome figures outside in the garden. I have a gargoyle on my bookshelf. If he sees something scary, he'll read about it to learn more. I let him watch *Legacy*, which is rated TV-14, due to language and situations. Some of the material is for an older audience. I fast forward through the kissing scenes. He asks me, "Why can't I see them kissing?"

"Because they're going to do more than kissing."

If he gets too scared, he'll sleep in our room, but he's too big for the bed, so he sleeps on the floor. Now that he's older, I can talk things over with him. "What are you scared of?"

"Monsters."

"Look, you got gnomes outside, so if anything gets through the perimeter, the gnomes will take 'em out. If it gets inside, the gargoyle's got it."

"Okay."

I don't curse at my son. If he's out of bounds, I say, "Hey, what are you doing?"

"Well, Mommy, I thought this."

"You thought wrong."

One time he was playing with his friends in the rose bushes. "What are you doing in the rosebushes?"

"We're getting pollen."

"What are you? Bees? Are you making honey? You don't need pollen. Now the bees don't have any pollen because you took all the pollen. Buzz off!"

It was more stressful when Flynn was younger. Kjell had reserve duty and I had to put Flynn in day care for a couple of hours each day. It was agonizing. You can do everything right and something can still happen to your child. Parents have to learn there are things outside their control. There are things I'd like to protect him from, but I don't. I'll tell him not to touch the hot stove and he'll touch it and burn his fingers. I don't yell at him or say, "I told you so." We have an expression in our house. "Life lesson. Next time, listen." Then I just walk away. It's painful to do that, but kids remember that way.

When Flynn was four years old we were at a playground. I saw this toddler walking toward the swings. He was about to get hit by the kids in the swings and of course he was oblivious. I ran up and grabbed him before he was booted into next week. Flynn saw it and said, "Wow, that kid almost had a life lesson."

## WHEN THREE BECOME FOUR

We started talking about expanding our family a couple of years ago. But I told Kjell, "This body may look like it can breed, but nothing else is coming out unless it's fibroids."

I had those taken out last year. So we looked into adoption.

The reason why we decided to have Maliya is because my husband and I, we've done very well and we have been successful and we wanted to give a child who was dealt a poor hand and maybe on a path to to something not so great, the opportunity to be the best human being that they can possibly be.

And we have the energy and time to do that, especially now that I'm retired. We knew that Flynn was this energetic, strong human being that can absorb some of it and still be able to deal with and be confident enough that if we put a little more attention to her that he would be okay. So That's why we decided.

Adoption is a lengthy process. It takes a year to build a file, check your references, assess your suitability to be adoptive parents. I told them, "I just retired from the military. I have top clearance."

We'd get presented with certain kids. Most people think - "Oh I want a baby for adoption, I want to do this or that." But, how does it change the whole family dynamics? We had to take that into consideration, because we're very stable family.

So now we're bringing someone else in this could be very catastrophic, this can tear families apart. So we had to be really mindful and thoughtful about how it's gonna affect each of us. After weighing all the considerations, we decided that our family would be complete with one more child.

So, we took the leap.

Kjell says, "You're usually the one who says no."

Maybe, but I'm also the one who has to bear the brunt of the work. I didn't want the dynamics of our family to change for the worse or have Flynn affected negatively.

In September 2020, we adopted a little girl, Maliya, younger than Flynn. We're committed to providing a household that is a steady home for Maliya, that's very important because she has had a very tumultuous life up until recently.

It's been quite an adjustment for our family. As PJ O'Rourke says, "Having one kid is like having a dog. Having two kids is like running a zoo."

# RACE RELATIONS

THE PEOPLE in my community are affluent professionals, upwardly mobile and very involved with their kids.

Moms will tell me, "Johnny is doing this program, and he's doing so well in gymnastics, and I started reading Harry Potter to him, and he's watching all the movies."

It's great to be proud of your kids, but I don't assume everybody is anxiously awaiting a daily progress report on my children's academic, fitness and cultural achievements.

The moms I'm friends with are the ones who are honest and say, "I'm a hot mess and I don't know what to do." We all are. The first essential for making good choices is to be comfortable with who you are. If you can't be that, you won't succeed. I know I'll never be one of the yoga pants mafia.

But there is much to like about my community. I like the school system. I like the house we live in. Which is not to say there isn't racism here. Maybe that's why we own our house.

## FINDING A HOME

When I was looking at places to rent, I went with the property manager to see a house. He left and I stayed a little longer to check it out. I got in my car and stopped at the stop sign at the entrance to the cul-de-sac to see where I was going next.

One of the neighbors came out of his house, got in his car, and approached me from the opposite direction. He rolled down his window. I rolled down my window. He said, "Can I help you?"

"No." I was looking at the directions on my phone.

"You don't live around here."

*Yeah, that's why I'm looking at my map* - I thought.

"Do you need some help getting out of the area?"

"No." He now had my undivided attention.

"Are you lost?"

"No, I'm good."

This conversation went on for about a minute, including awkward silences. Finally, we parted. I called the property manager on the phone. "I want to rent that house."

"Sure. I just need $30 to do a background check."

What is this bullshit? Background check? I was still mad about the racist neighbor. I did something I had never done before. "Just google me."

There was another awkward silence on the phone. "What?"

"Google me and call me back."

The property manager and I later became friends. He told me he looked me up on the web and saw my background and resume. He didn't even call me back. He called the owners of the house. "Have I got a tenant for you!"

We ended up renting that house. Every time I'd see that neighbor when I was jogging on the street, I'd just stare him down. He'd just look at me. He short sold his house about six months later. That was an indication that the neighborhood was improving, so we bought the house we were renting about six months after that.

White people feel awkward because they don't know how to act around people of color. They don't want to offend, they don't want to seem insensitive. White people should just say how they feel. If you feel awkward, just say you feel awkward. If you ask me how you should act, I don't know how you should act. If you ask how you can help, teach your kids to be open minded, not to be swayed by what social media and the news puts out.

When you're in the system, you have a cultural foundation, especially if you've been in it for many years. You may not even be aware of it. Just like in the military you have this culture ingrained in you over time. Some people are corrupt. Some are virtuous and rise above it. A lot of people are just listening to politicians and media, not thinking for themselves.

## BEING BLACK IN AMERICA

People talk about how black people have been oppressed. Yes, there has been oppression, particularly against black people. But people rise above it, they achieve despite the obstacles. Look at Colin Powell, Condoleeza Rice, people who just excel because they enjoyed the job. If you look at black doctors or black lawyers, or black military professionals, most came from backgrounds that weren't the best. We weren't defeated by the narrative. We just wanted to be better. We saw something we wanted and said, why can't we do it? We just need to say it more often. There's a lot of self doubt generated among people of color and women. Don't buy into the victimization. Your destiny is in your hands.

• • •

The word accountability has become inflammatory. We must hold ourselves accountable. I said that to a black friend a couple days ago and he said, "Why am I the only one accountable? Why can't white people be held accountable?" Sometimes you just gotta get out of your own damn way. You can only control how you conduct yourself and how you respond to the situation.

## EQUALITY OF OPPORTUNITY

People say that there's no equity or equal opportunity; we need more of this, more of that, we need to be heard. There is opportunity and we are being heard. Black people have brought so much to our culture. Rappers from the 90s are now actors on *CSI*. The talk of socio-economic oppression overshadows our achievements. I want to show people they can get out there and go after challenging jobs and work their butts off and accomplish something. Life is tough, but it's even tougher if you don't try. There are so many opportunities - don't waste them.

We have broken families. We have black men incarcerated at a rate that's insane. We have data that shows that if you're illiterate, the odds of you going to jail are exceedingly high, regardless of race. We know how to break the poverty cycle. Graduate from high school. Get a job. Do not have kids out of wedlock. Are these things hard to do? Yes. But they're essential.

I want to use fitness as an avenue to reach kids who are underserved. I want to get kids from different backgrounds and different economic circumstances to interact and promote an exchange of commonalities, ideas, thoughts and biases. That's how people understand and improve. I want to establish a place where this can happen. Profit, non-profit, I don't care, as long as we can provide services to help kids out of this rut, to break the cycle.

· · ·

People ask, why can't I have free health care? Why can't I have free this or free that? I come from a place where I busted my ass to obtain what I wanted. I share what I want to share because I earned that. Getting a free ride is not a good thing. There must be competition, there will always be winners and losers. Striving to do better makes us stronger. There is growth in the struggle.

We only get better by striving and failing and learning that the only way forward is not giving up. I was talking religion with a guy I work out with. The life of Jesus is all about struggle and sacrifice and resurrection. He came back better. If you're a functioning person, even with physical and mental limitations, you can strive and do well.

*None of us are trapped.*
*Some of us just have to work harder to escape.*

There's a lot of talk now about inequality.

What does that mean?

When you are doing something the best way you can, does that action in itself create inequality with others? When I was growing up I wanted to be an astronaut, like a lot of other kids. Did my effort toward that goal create inequality between me and those who didn't put in the same effort?

We should have equality of opportunity, not equality of outcome. Give everyone the same opportunity in life and let people fail or succeed. But you can't say we're gonna make the results equal across the board because it won't happen. Some will put in the effort to do better and others won't. I think of myself growing up. Why was I successful? Why did I get to do what I wanted to do? I was given some opportunities. Not at one point did I sit back and say, "Naw, I'll let this one pass." My attitude was always, "Let's do this. Let's go." If there were times that an opportunity didn't present itself I looked around until I found one.

# MY NEXT STEPS

*Get uncomfortable with it.*

MEMORIAL DAY IS close to my birthday, May 30th. This year, maybe I'll bike over to the veterans cemetery and hang out with the dead soldiers and airmen.

"Hey guys, what's up?"

I'm not scared of cemeteries. They're peaceful places to pay our respects. Arlington is great for that. There are so many who have given their lives. I just want to let them know it was worth it.

Speaking for myself, I want to be cremated. I don't want to take up space on this earth. If I could put my urn on a space flight and just release my ashes that would be cool. I'd do that. I believe that once your vessel is done, it's done. We're not getting reincarnated or coming back as zombies or any weird shit like that.

My husband surprised me for my 39th birthday, and that was okay. I don't have a favorite birthday, not in terms of a blowout. I'm a big fan of yellow or white cake, with white butter creme in between, with dark chocolate frosting. I like creamy fudge, but don't give me chocolate cake. I can tolerate it, but yellow cake is the best. My mom made the best home-made cakes. You know, Duncan Hines. We're from the Bronx, that's how we roll.

Nowadays we go over the top for my son's cakes. He likes yellow cake with vanilla frosting. It started when he was a one-year-old. When he was two it was a Paw Patrol cake.

Then my son started to like scary stuff, so the cake for his fifth birthday had a skull on top. For his sixth birthday, the cake was out of control. We got a Christine McConnel type of cake. She's known as the "goth baker" and she has her own Netflix show. She does elaborate, weird decorations, very macabre. We had a cake done of the house and a spider - it cost like two hundred bucks. It took us a month to eat it. We had to freeze it. If we spend money anywhere, we'll spend money on the cake.

## SOLO TRIPS TO VEGAS

My favorite indulgence right now is a twice-yearly solo trip to Vegas. I love my family, but I need days where I can get up when I want, walk around naked, have a Red Bull for breakfast and not have to worry about a husband, kids, cats, or anything operational in the house. I'm only responsible for me and no one else. Kjell's good with that. He knows when I go to Vegas, it's not with him.

I stay at the same hotel at the end of the strip every time. All the rooms are suites and each one has a huge soaker tub. I put in a whole bunch of bath salts that smell really nice, fill it up and sit in there for quite a while. There's a TV in there and I watch *Golden Girls*, probably because my grandmother liked the show. I have all seven seasons on DVD.

It's a non-smoking property. The interior has offset lighting, white sheets, very clean. But I always take some scouring powder because I don't like getting into a tub in a hotel that's not clean to my specifications. I can't take it in the container because of the TSA three ounce limit. So, I put the white powder in a little ziploc bag. But now I'm afraid if they go through my checked luggage they'll think it's cocaine.

I love the workout facility because you don't have to pay extra. I can go in there and work out for two hours. I usually get resort credit so I can go to the spa if I want to. I can sit in the four-person jacuzzi all by myself. It's as big as half a lane in a pool, so I can just chill out. There's a cold waterfall, hot steam, cold steam, showers.

I went to the Mandalay Bay aquarium to do the shark dive. I usually do some kind of excursion out there. Last time I was in Vegas was in February of 2020, right before I went to speak at the Air Force Museum in Ohio.

Gambling is a sin, but I enjoy it. I like playing against the odds because winning that one jackpot feels so damn good. You gotta risk it to get the biscuit. But don't gamble what you can't afford to lose. It leads to other addictions.

When I'm at home, being the paragon of fitness and nutrition, I have grape nuts and berries for breakfast, maybe a couple of pieces of toast for lunch, and sausage, peppers and mashed potatoes for dinner. Sometime I have pizza with shrimp or caviar - I picked up that habit in the Middle East. But when I'm in Vegas, I'm off the chain. There's a big buffet called Bacchanal at Caesar's Palace. I can spend four hours in there, being a total glutton. Usually I eat all the crawfish. The chefs see me walk in and say, "You eat all the crawfish." Yeah, keep it coming. I'll go to town and eat six plates of crawfish. It's so disgusting.

Sometimes I go to this place called Roku about two miles off the strip. I saw it on the Travel Channel. It's small, about the size of a three car garage. It opens at five in the afternoon, and doesn't close till three in the morning. No reservations. First come first served. If you're not there when the doors open you will not get a seat. They don't really have a menu. They get fresh catch every day, Langostino lobster, stuff like that. They have a sushi chef.

You can pay $75 per person and they'll give you different dishes, like tapas and some of the best tofu dishes.

When I go to Vegas, it's usually a three or four day trip. I have to plan ahead because Kjell has to take time off to stay home. We did a family trip there in November of 2020 for a wedding. So, I need to plan another solo trip. Kjell wanted to go. I said, "No, you cannot. This whole state's for me."

I'd rather do a family trip to South Dakota, because I want to see Mt. Rushmore. But Vegas just isn't big enough for both of us.

Family vacations are for bonding.

Traveling with my mom is also something I enjoy.

But, my solo trips to Vegas are sacred self-care.

## SECOND CAREER

*I won't stop until my body fails.*

Ever since I read the Jack Lalanne article in the U2 over the Mediterranean, I've been interested in being a personal trainer. After I retired I had time to do that. I started working at a local gym as a fitness coach and personal trainer.

If you're my client, you and I will jump some rope for a couple of minutes. That will get your heart rate up.

People tell me, "I can do a hundred burpees." But, they jump rope for three minutes and it's a wrap. I can turn the intensity up on anything for anyone at any age and it doesn't have to be burpees. I like to break it down and make sure you exercise each individual area of the body safely. Then we go into the dynamic portion. I can make you do waves on a forty foot battle rope in the squatted position for twenty seconds and it will crush your soul. It's not as hard an impact on the body.

· · ·

There's a trainer that used to work at our gym. She didn't like me. She used to run classes she called "Super High Intensity Training." She called them SHIT classes and she was right.

Fitness isn't about wrecking your body.

How many plyo boxes do you want to jump?

If you're over 40, do you really want to do plyo boxes?

You can do that stuff short term, like if you're preparing for a competition. But if you're just trying to get in shape, you dial it back. It's a marathon, not a sprint.

My general manager allows me a lot of leeway. He'll say, "Merryl, what do you think?"

And I'll tell him, "You don't pay me enough to think."

My boss allows me to do what I need to do. I try not to make waves unless somebody gets in my business, then the warrior of limitless fury comes out. An assistant manager was being pretty rude to me, so I just ignored her, wouldn't even talk to her. It sort of freaked her out. Finally, she says, "We need to talk." So we talked and I broke it down in a very direct way. She was pissed.

I was told that she went to the boss and said, "Either Merryl goes or I go."

If it comes down to a choice between her and me, it's going to be her. She was running her mouth and didn't know her position in the work place. As a trainer, I bring in clients, I increase traffic. I'm a moneymaker for the gym. She's an hourly employee. Nobody comes to the gym because it has a great assistant manager. She's a money loser. She didn't understand the environment.

It took her a month of being butt hurt, but then she started talking to me. "Oh, Merryl is really nice."

Yeah, no shit I'm nice.

I'm a nice person.

But don't be rude and disrespectful. I still carry the history of a colonel and there are certain things I won't put up with. Disrespect is one of them.

I have clients of all ages. One is a 76 year-old lawyer. He's been with me two-and-a-half years. He has a plane, we've flown together. I've trained his wife as well. She made me zucchini bread and blueberry cobbler. I like to build relationships.

The lawyer enjoys a trainer who can have an intelligent conversation and challenge him and get his quirky jokes. Sometimes he'll be dropping F-bombs and we can talk like we're in the military. I'll play music, and he's like, "What is this bullshit? I want to hear fight music." I have to play D12 or Eminem for him. Dude, you're off the chain. He's Jewish, so we talk about civil rights stuff. He puts off some of the other trainers because he's both cerebral and rough around the edges. He's a reserve judge. I still tell him to do push ups. For his 76th birthday I made him do 76 push-ups, throughout the workout.

"Why am I doing so many?"

"Because you're 76 today. Happy Birthday."

*Don't be afraid of tomorrow. Embrace it.*

Some of my clients who are over 60 still think they're in 30 year-old bodies. I show them very quickly that's not the case. You may not be 30 but I will work you hard. I do more balance work, more strength training to maintain bone density. Some women are pre-menopausal, like me, so we laugh about hot flashes. Some will say, "If I laugh too hard, I might pee a little." The struggle is real.

When twenty-year-old guys come to train with me, I'll run them into the ground. Two rounds of jump rope with stuff in between. If I did that with my 76 year old, I'd have to get the defibrillator.

. . .

The reason I picked this gym was that it had an older clientele. Older clientele means more disposable income. I don't want to run around with twenty-year-olds who train for a month, then look cool and leave. I want to train people with some longevity. I have a 64-year-old client who comes from a family where no one lives past 65. He's ornery, he was in the Army, so sometimes I give him a hard time.

I'll tell him to do ten pushups, and he'll be doing them, and say, "How many is that?"

"It's eight. Oh, I forgot, you're Army. Do you need me to count slower?" He flips me off and then does the exercise.

After 60, muscle mass drops off and balance goes. My clients say, "I didn't know this was happening. Why is this happening?" This is how the Grim Reaper comes into your life. First you lose muscle mass. Then you lose your balance. You become frail, you walk down the stairs, you slip and fall and break your hip. You become sedentary. It happens to all of us.

It's critical to keep moving. Movement is life. Strengthen those areas. "Well, when I was in my fifties, I was lifting 135." Well now you're in your 70s, let's back that off, let's start here. And we'll work on it. You have to manage their expectations.

I'll put my older clients in a chair and watch them get up. They'll start trying to rock and use their hands. I won't let them get away with that.

I tell them to cross their arms and get up. "Put your feet down, feel your toes, the soles of your feet, push through your heels, brace your core as you're coming up." They'll do three sets of ten and be sweating and embarrassed. But it's coming for all of us.


I have a retired cop, 78, he does boxing with me, once a week for 45 minutes. His reflexes are slow but he punches hard. He told me he was out in this area where there were a lot of meth addicts, which he calls "zombies."

He said, "Merryl, you taught me these movements, and I was on the street when this zombie came up and looked like he was going to rush me. I put up my hands in the boxing position and he just backed off." Fitness builds confidence.

## STRATEGIC PLANNING FOR A SUCCESSFUL LIFE

On my website, I offer strategic planning for a successful life. The conduit is fitness. Sometimes you work out so hard you have this moment of clarity. I push people to that point. My older clients have already done that. We exchange stories and ideas and we just talk. That's fun. They're baby boomers and they have a different perspective.

Some of my younger clients may not know what they want or how to achieve it. I use fitness to make a connection. Some want to join the military. I say, "Okay, let's see your pull up." If they can't do a pull up, we got a problem. If you want to go to a service academy, you have to do push ups, pull ups, an overhead throw. The military wants to see upper body strength.

Some parents send their kids to me because they want somebody positive in their kids' lives. One of my clients is my neighbor's son. He got his pilot's license before he could drive. We'd work out together. He wanted to join the military, so I took him out to Beale to show him the base. In between sets, I'd answer his questions.

The principal of Flynn's school reached out to me because her niece wants to be a military pilot. I worked out with her, we talked about what she wanted to do. She went over to the Navy, got picked up for the pilot program, so she'll go to OCS and flight school.

Trust is a high priority. My clients trust me to show them how to work out in a safe manner. We sit down and interview first. They tell me personal and medical information. The more I know about you, the more effective the training can be. A female prospective client said, "Why do you need to do that?" Because I want to make your experience as beneficial as possible. I don't want to give you something that will hurt you later down the road.

One of my first clients, a teenager, suffered from anxiety and depression. Fitness is great for people with those issues. I worked with him about a year, during which time he was also seeing a therapist. He started playing basketball. I taught him some basic martial arts and his confidence level went up. He had been a home school kid, but now he started going to school. He had to see his therapist less and less. His mom became a friend. For a mother to trust me with her son, and for him to trust me enough so that I can help him succeed, that meant a lot.

I'd like to talk more to underserved kids. A lot of kids aren't motivated because they don't have the means. They're living at or below the poverty line. They don't have access to things. They're just going to have to hustle harder. Kids from single parent households are on their own because a parent has to work and pay bills. They're just ripping and running with their friends, doing things they're not supposed to because that's all they know.

If I can get to those kids and say, "Hey, there's another way. But that means you're going to have to stay home and grab a book and learn how to freaking read. Start hanging out with people who look at life differently."

That's why I think about the gym so much. How can I use the gym to access kids like that?

## THE OTHER SIDE

At the gym, the clientele is mostly wealthy. That's not always an advantage for kids, either. This eleven-year-old kid was mouthing off to one of the female staff members at the gym, disrupting other kids who were doing homework, making obscene gestures, showing off for his buddies. The staff member warned him to shape up or she'd call his mom. His response was, "Go ahead, I don't care."

I couldn't resist. I stepped in and told him, "Why don't you pick up a McDonald's application on the way out? You'd be perfect." His friends cracked up, which made him mad.

He challenged me, "Do you want to fight?"

I said, "I already won." They cracked up again, and now he was in tears because he'd been humiliated in front of his friends.

Club management told me I had to talk to the parents. The mom of this kid called, telling me how I emasculated him, how I bullied an eleven-year-old child. She was rationalizing the kid's behavior. She wanted an apology. I gave her my perspective which was when an eleven-year-old makes sexual remarks to an adult staff member, makes obscene gestures and challenges another staff member to a fight, he's no longer an eleven-year-old kid. If he pulled that kind of stuff in the Bronx he'd get his teeth knocked out. I gave him a life lesson he wasn't getting at home.

## THE VIDEO THAT TURNED TO TV

Sometimes when I work with a client, I will use video to review the session. In January of 2020, I had my phone set up to record a boxing workout. While I was waiting for my client, I recorded myself dancing in the gym, just some warmup moves, about twenty seconds. I later posted that video on Facebook.

I received positive reactions and comments, including one that said, "I sent you an email about a project you should be part of." Naturally, I thought it was a sales pitch or a scam. So I checked out the sender, Jenny Hope, and found out she was a producer and casting director. I got in touch with her and she told me she had seen my video, then researched my background. She was casting for a reality show on CBS called *Tough As Nails*, and wanted me to be part of it.

There was an interview process and certain physical requirements because they told me the show made rigorous demands on the contestants. I qualified, and then went to work preparing for the challenges ahead.

Part of *Tough As Nails* is team competition. Teamwork is hard. You have to get along with people you don't necessarily like. Just like in the military you have to work with people to accomplish the mission and sometimes people are dicks, so it can be very difficult. You have to have meetings. You have to put your personal biases aside - family, personal baggage, false beliefs, life experiences. You gotta figure out how to work with people you might have nothing in common with and still be effective. That's difficult.

When you're working by yourself it's just you against the obstacle. There's immediate feedback and you can't blame anyone else if you fail. In teamwork you have to work together and when one of your teammates is struggling, you lend support and vice-versa. You build camaraderie and strengthen that social network which in the end is good for everybody, as opposed to being a lone warrior of limitless fury. But teamwork is hard.

When I was watching the Super Bowl in 2021, right after half-time, a promo for *Tough As Nails* came on. They used one of my quotes that said, "I'm doing this for all the girls of color."

My phone exploded. Throughout the rest of the game I had texts and calls from all kinds of people, some I hadn't spoken to in fifteen years. "Was that you?"

I wouldn't do a reality show if they were going to make me the evil, bitchy person. That's not me. I can't be something I'm not.

The show is about how far people will go, physically and mentally, to get the job done. I saw the trailer for the first season, teams were doing stuff like shoveling 3000 pounds of dirt, doing real jobs. I thought, I can do this. All I gotta do is put one foot in front of the other. I'd just like to see how far I can push myself.

I read *Can't Hurt Me* by David Goggins, a Navy SEAL who had a crappy start in life. He went from SEAL training to running 100 miles for a marathon without even prepping for it. He went through BUDS and Hell week two or three times with a busted kneecap and all this other stuff, but he kept running through the pain. I read that story and I thought, you're a dumb ass. But if I'm honest with myself, I'd probably do the same thing. I laugh because I get it. I understand pushing yourself to see how far you can go.

On *Tough As Nails,* I knew I might not be number one, but I would strive for that. I'm quietly competitive. I come on like, "Aw, you don't have to worry about me." But deep inside I've already scoped out the room and know who I have to beat. I've always done that.

## ME, AS A SPEAKER

In 2016, when I was still in the Air Force, I was invited to Idaho to speak at the Women in Leadership conference at the Andrus Center. There was an informal dinner before the conference where the speakers met the hosts. I was at a table, talking and joking a little bit, and I said, "I didn't realize I was branding myself, like Kim Kardashian without the sex tape." And they all thought that was the most hilarious thing. I can get away with cracks like that. That's my swagger. I'm a little funny.

I was the keynote speaker the last day of the conference. I was nervous - there were 700 people in the audience. I wanted to sound normal, but I wasn't sure what they wanted to hear. Well,

I just got up and told my story like I was talking to somebody across the table from me and I knocked it out of the park.

But it was weird to have people come up afterward with these starry looks in their eyes, like I just revealed something amazing. It freaked me out because I didn't know I could bring out that type of emotion in people. It was surreal. They invited me back a year-and-a-half later to talk at a smaller forum. They appreciated me out there and I think even to this day they still talk about my speech.

It turns out I enjoy speaking. It's different than addressing people under my command. Talking to people you don't know and who have never seen you is more demanding. There's a piece of myself that I give to the audience. I'm emotionally tired after I talk.

When I talk about my life, I get various reactions. One of my friends said, "You're a force of nature. You can do things other people can't do."

Why? Am I a superhero?

I believe anyone can succeed with the right motivation. To motivate people, you just have to be aware of your surroundings and understand people.

If there's a guy on the verge of tears, screaming at him is not going to help. If someone is very religious, swearing at him will not be effective. But if it's a military person who's been in for twenty years, I might be able to throw a whole bunch of F-bombs in there and really fire him up. It just takes a moment to get to know someone. If you're a little bit giving and receptive to other people, you can figure out how to motivate them. I morph to fit the circumstances. I've yelled at people, cried with people, joked with people - every person is different.

•  •  •

I like talking about leadership. People read all these leadership books, they'll talk about different techniques, but they can't put those techniques into action. I've read books on leadership like *Servant Leader* and Sun Tzu's *The Art of War*. I've done Air Command and Staff College and Air War College and read about different approaches of military leaders. There are some good ideas you can use. But the key remains that you have to be able to read people and learn what gets them going. It's not about manipulation. It's about figuring out how to motivate people and inspire them to achieve the objective.

Those closest to me may see this whirlwind of crazy activity, dancing on the table of my office or yelling on the phone one minute, then quietly encouraging and counseling a subordinate the next - different approaches for different people. I do whatever it takes to get that person to make the maximum contribution to accomplish a goal.

You have to get to know individuals to be able to lead them. It doesn't take much effort to remember something about some one on your team or learn a person's name or job. You walk down the hall and say, "How's aircraft number such and such?" It shows that you know what they're working on and they appreciate that. They know they're not anonymous to you.

"How was your weekend, did you catch anything?" That person thinks; *Oh, the commander knows I went fishing this weekend.*

Those little things build a relationship. That's what motivates people. Feeling wanted and respected is huge. It pays big dividends. You can do that in one sentence, in the way you greet some one or ask a question.

I don't have a six-step program on how to be a great leader. I just know how to be effective. And part of that is being a mentor as well as a leader. A mentor is some one who's more hands-on to help you get to a goal.

. . .

A leader is direct. He'll say, "Go take that hill!", and he'll expect you to do it. A mentor may show you different ways to take that hill. "You can take it from underneath, fly over the top and take it, take it from the side, you can walk it, or maybe we need to use a boat. I'll help you get that boat and we'll row over there together."

## MENTORSHIP

*If you not mentoring, you're wrong.*

I mentor the kids who are my clients. I found out one kid was a baseball player who wanted to get into the business side of the game. I asked him, "How would it be if I set up a meeting for you with a scout from the Mets?" He was knocked out. "Here's his number. His son and my son go to school together." That's how mentors work.

I also want kids to know they don't have to do it on their own. Everybody likes to think of themselves as a spectacular person. But you typically need someone in your corner to help you. I've had more than my fair share of people who've helped me, or kept me out of trouble, or had my back when I got into trouble. It's not a problem to pick up a phone and call some one or text some one and say, "Hey, can you help this kid out?"

Mentorship requires proximity. It's like Newton's Law of gravitational force. The force is greater the closer the objects are to each other. When I was a kid, my dad was so far away, his gravitational pull was minimal. He was too distant to have any pull. But others who were closer have greater impact. I'm the sum of all my mentors. My mom was a constant guiding force. She was close by, sometimes too close, but she had a tremendous positive influence on my life. My grandmother was a huge influence because of how much time I spent with her. In junior high,

Mr. Russo was a mentor, and Mr. Lieb in high school. In college, Dr. Morrison picked me up and drove me to the University of Maine. He treated me like one of his daughters. General Shanahan was my mentor. We're all products of our experiences and whom we interact with. Being a mentor is an important responsibility and I never take it lightly.

I was talking about long-term goals with a friend of mine who has some lofty ambitions. I asked him how he planned to achieve them. He said, "I'm just going to be open to whatever the universe presents to me."

"That's a load of bullshit. And you know it." He wasn't prepared for that reaction, nor for the follow-up.

"What are you gonna do to make it happen? What are three measurable milestones on the path to success? Give me details, let me see your plan, show me what you've done so far."

Like I said before, hope is not a career strategy. Have a plan. Move the ball. Get it done.

People don't like to identify their goals because that holds them accountable. They avoid that because if they fail, they can say, "Oh, the universe didn't want me to have that." No, you gotta go friggin' get it, you jackass.

I think Americans have lost that drive to succeed. My mom wanted to give me more than what she had, her mother wanted to give her more than what she had. Now people think, "I'm just gonna sit back and it's gonna come to me." That's cowardly.

You're not going to succeed in everything. Part of growth is failing and learning what type of person you truly are. Everyone goes through it. It's how you come out on the other side, how you react, that determines who you are.

I did a zoom meeting with some kids at virtual space camp.

One of them asked, "What's it like to fly the U2?"

The U2 is a phenomenal aircraft that still performs the mission it was designed to do in the middle of the last century. But I feel about the U2 the same way I feel about other aircraft. The U2 doesn't care who you are. It doesn't care what color your skin is, what neighborhood you're from, or how rich you are. The only thing the aircraft cares about is whether or not you can fly. Inanimate objects just have one criterion, and there is no bias. You're either good at using them or you're not. You're either a good pilot or you're a bad pilot. Get in the cockpit and let's see if you've got what it takes. This is not subjective. It's a dangerous machine if handled improperly. You can hurt yourself, you can crash, you can eject. You can get killed. And that's okay because I enjoy that challenge.

Some people live a lifetime in a little box, scared to set foot outside. Being born is not your choice and death is inevitable. What you do in between is up to you. I'm not saying I want to go out in a blaze of glory. But I would like to go out knowing that I aimed high, worked hard, and maybe inspired others to do the same.

THE END?

NOT EVEN CLOSE

# CHARITABLE PARTNER

Partial Proceeds of the sale of this book go to Legacy Flight Academy ™.

LFA is a non-profit organization that conducts character-based youth aviation programs that draw upon the legacy of the Tuskegee Airmen. Our comprehensive three-tiered approach works in tandem with partner organizations to help minorities and underrepresented youth achieve success as aerospace and STEM professionals, particularly emphasizing military career opportunities.

**What We Do**

LFA's comprehensive three-tiered approach provides awareness, inspires interest, offers features engaging activities and delivers ongoing opportunities for youth to understand and pursue aero-space careers. Although minority youth figure strongly in our outreach, participation in LFA programs is open to all students, just as the legacy of the Tuskegee Airmen transcends any ethnic, racial or gender barrier.

Furthermore as exemplified by the Tuskegee Airmen, we emphasize the critical importance of strong character as the requirement for success, regardless of an individual's ultimate career goal.

# ACKNOWLEDGMENTS

This book could not have been possible without the community of people who supported me along the way.

Mr. Ronnie Robinson, was my on-wing and mentor. He taught me how to fly. He instilled the foundational skillset of what it means to be a pilot in me. When you get in an aircraft you put everything in it - all your focus, attention. There is no room for error. The aircraft will kill you if you mess around. You showed me that as an officer, you teach people and mentor them.

Lance Thompson, thank you so much for going on this writing journey with me. Lance is incredibly talented, you took my voice and edited it on the page to keep my style and keeping my "New York-ness". I have nothing but reverence for Lance and his work ethic.

Chris Hopkins for using your incredible "skillz" in creating my amazing portrait that now resides in the Pentagon and the cover of this book.

Elisabeth Farrell, thank you for you friendship and support throughout the decades. Not only do I trust Liz with my story, but also as the Godmother to my son. I have nothing but the highest level of respect for her and her opinion.

Ken Hall for being my son's Godfather. Your friendship was one of the first to teach me the intel side of the U2. I trust Ken implicitly. I thank you for your mentorship and tutelage throughout the years.

To my mentors: Mrs. Harriet, Mr. Russo, Mr. Leib, Mr. Feldman, Mr. Buchaltz, Mrs. Mostovoy, Dr. Morris, Dr. Morrison, Capt

Dana Gordon, USN (ret.), Col Michael "Dog" Senna, USAF (ret.), Lieutenant General Stayce Harris, USAF (ret.), Lieutenant General John "Jack" Shannahan, USAF (ret.). You helped guide me through my journey. You were so pivotal in making a positive influence in my life. I cannot thank you enough.

Dr. Marilyn Croach, one of my early mentors, and Tad Thompson, thank you for your persistence in pushing me to write my story.

Lucinda Rae, thank you for your phenomenally artistic eye for the design of my book cover.

Merav Richter of Maverick Productions Inc., I'm so glad our paths crossed. From our first meeting, I knew that you were the right person. I'm so grateful that you were able to take my journey and my book to a level that makes such an impact on so many people.

My friend and Gemini twin Jennifer Cory who, after making fun of my title suggestions came up with an amazing phrase. Thank you so much for your friendship at a time when I most needed it.

My friend Felix Ucan who's is always there to capture all the wonderful shots of my life.

To my mom, I thank you for putting up and tolerating my crazy ass. You let me be myself. I'm very appreciative that I've been successful at being me. I'm glad you let me be my authentic self.

To my husband, Kjell, I'm so glad that I found such a strong guy to put up with me. Being married to me, and dating me, is not for the faint of heart. To be able to allow me to do me, and still be confident in what you do, doesn't rattle you at all. You have always supported me in all of it. You are a force to be reckoned with - you're just quiet about it. We are two forces together, in our own ways.

To my kids, Flynn and Maliya, you are the inspiration for the Life Lessons in this book. As you get older, what I'd like you to take away - whatever your origin is, just accept who you are, don't try to hide it. It's who you are that's going to make you successful. It doesn't mean that life is going to be easy for you, it's going to be challenging anyway, don't make it harder by NOT being you. Be you and find the people who are on the same path as you and are going in the same direction as you.

# ABOUT THE AUTHOR

Colonel **Merryl Tengesdal** is the first and only African American woman to fly the United States Air Force's U2 spy plane which is used for specialized high-altitude reconnaissance missions.

Merryl Tengesdal is a military veteran and former Director of Inspections who served for The Air Force Inspector General from October 2015 through August 2017. A retired United States Air Force Colonel, Tengesdal served in the Iraq War and the War in Afghanistan.

She now works as a fitness professional and motivational speaker.

In 2020, Merryl was a contestant on the TV show *Tough as Nails.*

She lives with her husband and two children in California.

Visit her website at www.MerrylTengesdal.com

Made in United States
Orlando, FL
18 September 2023

37051331R00145